Riv 1 189

Crime in America

1983

CRIME IN AMERICA
THE
(abc)
REPORT

THE

REPORT

by
Donald MacGillis and ABC News
Introduction by Richard Threlkeld

Developed by The Stonesong Press, Inc.
and Philip Lief and Associates

CHILTON BOOK COMPANY
Radnor, Pennsylvania

Photo Credits
Chapter One: (Al Capone.) UPI Photo
Chapter Two: (Condemned Bowery building.) UPI Photo
Chapter Three: (Prison hallway.) Mark Mellett Photography
Chapter Four: (Looted grocery store.) UPI Photo
Chapter Five: (Police confrontation at demonstration.) UPI Photo
Chapter Six: (Guardian Angels.) UPI Photo
Chapter Seven: (Courthouse.) George W. Gardner
Chapter Eight: (Prison cell.) Mark Mellett Photography
Chapter Nine: (Boy before window.) Mark Mellett Photography
Chapter Ten: (Man embracing woman.) UPI Photo
Chapter Eleven: (Guns on store shelf.) George W. Gardner
Chapter Twelve: (Family mourning.) UPI Photo

Published in Radnor, Pennsylvania 19089, by Chilton Book Company
Designed by Richard Glassman, Blackbirch Graphics
Library of Congress Catalog Card No. 83-70825
ISBN 0-8019-7401-1 *hardcover*
ISBN 0-8019-7402-x *paperback*
Manufactured in the United States of America

1 2 3 4 5 6 7 8 9 0   2 1 0 9 8 7 6 5 4 3

Contents

Introduction

or me, the single most exciting scientific revelation of the twentieth century was the discovery some years ago that radio waves have very special qualities. Unlike daffodils or squirrels or TV newscasters, radio waves are not bound by gravity, or much of anything else. They don't grow old, they don't die—they just sail out into space. Everything ever spoken on the radio, everything you ever saw go by on the TV, is still *out there* somewhere, chugging along through the cosmos, indefinitely. This is a heady realization for a newscaster. It affords a kind of comforting immortality. Even after you are long gone, all your old reruns will still be playing Somewhere East of the Milky Way.

That notion is particularly comforting for those in TV news. Necessarily ephemeral, news is on the screen long enough to inform and excite people, distress them or amuse them, and then it is gone. In an instant, it is older than yesterday's newspaper. So there is always a certain melancholy associated with any TV news effort. Every news program, every documentary, becomes a beloved child that must die in infancy.

What follows is a happy exception to that rule of TV news mortality. In the autumn of 1982, ABC News embarked on a reporting project quite unprecedented in network journalism. It was an examination of our nation's crime problem and the state of our criminal-justice system. It required eight months of the best work of hundreds of ABC newspeople, who covered the country. And when we finally put it on television, it occupied all or part of sixty hours of ABC-News programming during two weeks in February of 1983. We called it "Crime in America."

Crime is such a broad subject that, even with all that time and effort, we could deal with only one facet: crime against people and their property, better known as street crime. White-collar crime, organized crime and official corruption are all serious problems in this country. But what *most* frightens us as citizens (as we quickly discovered from the results of an ABC-News Crime Poll commissioned for the series) and what we as a nation spend so much of our time and resources fighting is violent crime—the work of the desperadoes among us.

The FBI, which measures that sort of thing, defines violent crime as the following: murder, rape, robbery, assault, burglary and car theft. Perhaps you've been luck enough not to have been a victim of any of the crimes on that list. Perhaps you've never walked out in the street to an empty space at the curb where your car used to be. Perhaps you've never opened the front door and felt that awful wrench in the pit of your stomach on discovering your home has been ransacked and everything in it that was really important to you has been expropriated by burglar or burglars unknown.

Perhaps not. But every living American—man, woman and child—has been frightened by a strange footfall on a lonely street or thought twice about passing by a dark corner or trembled for a moment at something that went bump in the night. This book has something to tell you.

Donald MacGillis, a talented author and editor, has done much more than simply snatch those sixty hours of TV journalism off the screen and put them into print. TV news is the prisoner of time. There's never enough air time to tell you everything we want to. ABC News interviewed hundreds of criminals and cops and judges and lawyers and criminologists in the course of making this series, and 90 percent of all that material wound up on the cutting-room floor. It always does. So Don MacGillis has taken the best of what we told you, and what we didn't have time to tell you, and combined it with his own research to fashion a primer on crime in America today.

Why is there so much crime in this country? Is it getting worse? Who are the criminals? Why can't the police ever seem to catch them? And if they do, why do the courts let them go? And if criminals do wind up behind bars, how is it they always seem to get out too soon? Will tougher laws, tougher punishment, more police stop crime? Is there any hope?

There are answers to all those questions in the pages that follow. You will find yourself surprised, intrigued and perhaps angered by what you discover on this journey through the mean streets, the precinct houses, the crowded courtrooms and the prison cellblocks of America. You'll also be somewhat wiser for taking the journey. We were.

And a little wisdom applied to our crime problem wouldn't hurt. Too often our national argument about it has been characterized more by heat than light. We're not the first nation to be afraid of the criminals among us—and confused about what to do about them. Three centuries ago, John Locke, the great English political philosopher who was as much an author of our Constitution as any of the Founding Fathers, offered some advice to his fellow citizens, then suffering through times far more violent and crime-ridden than our own.

A just and fair society, Locke observed, requires that no one do harm to another in his life, health, liberty or possessions. So criminals must be caught and punished, for the security of honest men and women. But punished, Locke cautioned, only "so far as calm reason and conscience dictate."

Calm reason and conscience are necessary ingredients in whatever we debate, whatever we finally do about Crime in America.

—Richard Threlkeld

Chapter 1

A nation of laws and outlaws

I came here in 1918, and people used to sleep
outdoors all night, especially in the summertime.
Used to go down on the river and sleep. But you can't
do it now. If you do you'll wake up and find yourself
dead.

—Lois Wade of Washington, D.C.

iolent crime—the stranger on the
street with a gun—is no stranger in American history. Yet, in what
historians Hugh David Graham and Ted Robert Gurr have called
a case of "historical amnesia," we have not owned up to this fact.
As a result, of all the myths and illusions that distort Americans'
views of criminal violence, the most deep-seated is certainly the
notion that the country is by nature a peaceful land inhabited by a
law-abiding Chosen People. Seen through this rose-colored lens,
the sharp rise in crime since the early 1960s appears to be a total
break from an innocent past in which law and order were taken
for granted as ground rules of the American Dream.

Nothing could be further from the truth. The United States has
an unacknowledged tradition of collective and individual lawbreaking that stands out among the industrialized countries.
Historians believe the reason that this tradition has not received

the attention it deserves from the public, government officials and scholars is because violence has rarely touched at the core of national political life. Notable exceptions are the Civil War and the attacks of assassins on presidents. Otherwise, uprisings have not challenged the federal government and, in turn, the federal government has—with the exception of the Indian wars—not used armed power against its own people in the manner of Nazi Germany or Stalin's Soviet Union.

But the fact that violence in this country has been spasmodic and generally isolated in its effects does not mean it has been unimportant in the nation's development. The most thorough-going attempt by historians to explore this dark side of American history came in the late 1960s when increases in street crime, race riots and antiwar violence forced the country to ask itself whether black militant Rap Brown was right when he said that violence is "as American as cherry pie." The answer of historians Richard Hofstadter and Michael Wallace in *American Violence* and Graham and Gurr in *The History of Violence in America* was a clear yes.

America's violent nineteenth century

In 1838, a young politician making his first important public speech in Springfield, Illinois, decried "the increasing disregard for law which pervades the country." It was Abraham Lincoln, addressing a problem that was, by 1838, already a rich source of American oratory: the danger posed to domestic tranquillity by criminals, gangs and mobs. In the decade before Lincoln made that speech, the mayor of Boston, Josiah Quincy, was once forced to personally lead a citizen posse to put down a riot that had gone on for a week. And it was only one of several during his term.

The nineteenth century was marked by brutal suppression of slave uprisings, anti-Irish mobs and enough bloody labor disputes to give the United States the dubious distinction of having the worst history of labor violence in the world. The first three decades of this century were, in some ways, even worse: By most measures, individual crime increased, and Prohibition helped to spawn organized crime.

Crime and Violence — part of U.S. past

Recalling the crime and violence of the nation's past is not done to minimize or explain away the problems of the present. The advantage of a historical perspective is that it teaches lessons about lawbreaking. The most important of these is that criminality and violence rise and fall according to a great number of factors, some of which can be affected by a concerned citizenry working inside or outside of government.

The situation is not hopeless. As recently as the late 1960s, for instance, there was fear that race riots might become a staple of the urban scene and that campus unrest might become a staple of the college scene. Although either phenomenon could reappear at any time, there are probably identifiable reasons that they have not. Inner-city tensions seem to have been eased by the integration of city police forces and by the impressive ability of black voters, usually working with whites, to elect black mayors in many of the country's biggest cities. As for campus disturbances, the success of the federal government in staying out of unpopular foreign wars in the last ten years has lowered the pitch of student activism dramatically.

Nonetheless, while historians can offer us comforting—or distressing—evidence that earlier periods in U.S. history experienced far more overall violence than ours, it is difficult for them to measure the level of criminal violence—murders, robberies, rapes—that earlier generations suffered. The most reliable statistics available are for murder, the one crime that is almost always reported to the police, as many crimes aren't.

By that one grim yardstick, the upsurge in crime that began in the 1960s was at least the equal of the crime boom of the first three decades of this century. In each, the rate of murder per 100,000 inhabitants climbed to near or above the ten milestone.

Unfortunately, that comparison almost certainly understates the relative size of the crime problem the nation is now facing. The crime data that the FBI first began collecting in 1933 indicate that property crime has risen substantially since that time.

A couple of cautionary notes are in order here. For crimes other than murder, those early FBI figures are not considered very reliable. Moreover, it is at least conceivable that property-crime incidence from the more lawless 1920s *greatly* exceeded the 1933 totals and may even approach the high levels of the recent past. But this seems unlikely. A fair conclusion would be that, in the twentieth century at least, the American public has never faced a higher rate of crime than it has in its most recent past. The encouraging news from the data is that the crime boom *appears* to have begun to abate in 1981 and 1982—the problem is serious but not, contrary to conventional wisdom, getting worse.

The industrialized world's leader in crime

Why the United States, why now? The first question is worth asking because there is no doubt that the United States leads the industrialized world in crime. While most other nations have seen their crime rates rise in the recent past, none even approaches the U.S. level. To use, once again, the most solid statistic: The U.S. murder rate is almost 10 per 100,000, Japan's is 1.6, Britain's is 1.3 and West Germany's is 1.3.

To explain why the United States is the world leader among developed countries in crime is to answer the question of what causes crime—something that criminologists have found extremely difficult to do. There is a whole list of pat explanations, virtually all of which can be refuted, at least in part, by contradictory evidence from the United States's own experience.

For instance, one frequently cited explanation for the high crime rate of the United States is that the process of urbanization—the transformation of the United States from a rural country into a largely city-dwelling one—was more traumatic and disruptive here than elsewhere. This theory may explain some of the nation's social problems, but a fascinating study of nineteenth-century criminal records in the state of Massachusetts by historian Roger Lane directly challenges the notion that the city is, by itself, a breeder of violent crime.

In his essay, "Urbanization and Criminal Violence in the Nineteenth Century: Massachusetts as a Test Case," Lane looked at four indices of crime in the state—the number of lower-court cases, jail commitments, grand-jury cases, and imprisonments—and found that they indicated a gradual per-capita decline in serious crime between 1834 and 1901 (figures for two of the indices, number of lower-court cases and jail commitments, were not available until 1860). The incidence of grand-jury cases fell by more than one-third during this time of rapid urbanization, the incidence of imprisonment by no less than 65 percent.

The trend evident in these court statistics cannot be simply explained away by saying that Massachusetts had grown less punitive during those decades. On the contrary, offenses that in the 1830s would have resulted in a two-year sentence were punished later in the century by three-to-four-year confinements. Also, society became much less willing to tolerate drunkenness and brawling as the century progressed. While the incidence of arrest for serious crimes clearly declined, the rate of arrests for more minor offenses against public order zoomed.

This evolution of Massachusetts from a largely rural, free-wheeling society to a more straitlaced, urban one was not, according to Lane, uninterrupted. According to his research, the one period when urbanization did not work its civilizing influence was in the twenty-five years immediately preceding the Civil War. During this time, the state—and especially Boston—was swamped by immigrants both from the New England countryside and also from Ireland, which was suffering the privation of the "hungry forties." Economic development during this time, he said, was "not fully able to keep pace with migration." And, "Without the discipline imposed by regular employment, this first large-scale flow of migrants into the city was a kind of mutual disaster."

The weight of Lane's evidence is that urbanization, far from spawning violent crime, will reduce it—*if* there is sufficient economic growth to absorb the immigrants into cities. That is an important qualification and may help to explain the consistently higher rates of crime in U.S. cities than in small towns or rural areas. But movement from the farm to the city need not in itself be associated with crime increases—if the city can offer gainful employment.

Another analysis of the problem is that crime has been accentuated in the United States by the difficulty of assimilating wave after wave of immigrants, many of whom have language problems that complicate their fitting into industrial society. There may be some merit to this notion, particularly for the second generation of immigrants whose behavior appears to be more affected by the trauma of growing up in a foreign environment. But it so happens that the section of the United States that has, over the decades, received the fewest immigrants and has in fact had the most stable society is the one that has been plagued by the highest rates of violent crime—the South.

A further explanation of the American weakness for violent crime is that it was fostered by the experience of living on civilization's frontier, with loosely enforced laws and a tradition of individuals taking the law into their hands to settle their own disputes. But other countries that have gone through a similar stage of development, such as Canada and Australia, do not have our crime problems. Moreover, some of the states that have had the highest rates of violent crime are, again, the southeastern ones, such as Georgia and the Carolinas, whose residents are generations removed from frontier life.

The fact that for decades residents of the South, both whites and blacks, have been committing violent crimes at rates noticeably higher than other Americans has led to some interesting inquiries that may shed light on the problem of criminality in the nation as a whole. Sheldon Hackney's essay, "Southern Violence," in *The History of Violence in America* suggests that the pattern may be attributable to the history of the South's Civil War defeat and its long period of economic stagnation. "Being Southern then," Hackney writes, "inevitably involves a feeling of persecution at times and a sense of being a passive, insignificant object of alien or impersonal forces. Such a historical experience has fostered a world view that supports the denial of responsibility and locates threats to the region outside the region and threats to the person outside the self." Hackney also suggests that blacks may have a similar world view born of years as second-class citizens.

Hackney's thesis points to another answer to the "Why America?" question—our tragic history of slavery and the long legal, political and economic subjugation of blacks. While the South may lead the nation as the region most plagued by violent crime, blacks, as a group, are responsible for the highest rates of this kind of crime. In 1981, blacks made up 45.7 percent of all those arrested for crimes of violence, a percentage way out of proportion to their 12 percent share of the population.

The explanations for this are, again, complex, but it is hard to quarrel with the conclusion of Charles E. Silberman, author of the insightful *Criminal Violence, Criminal Justice*, when he wrote: "If criminal violence is to be reduced to a tolerable level, those who now feel excluded must become full, participating members of American society with a major stake in its preservation." Silberman specifically calls for "the elimination of poverty, inequality and racial discrimination as significant factors in American life."

Our "gun culture"

One quite evident reason that the United States leads the industrialized world in crime is that it leads the world in the private ownership of one of criminals' favorite tools, the gun. In *American Violence* Richard Hofstadter writes: "Every aspect of violence in our history, from riots to presidential assassinations, has been exacerbated by the fact that ours is a gun culture—a thing without parallel among the industrial nations of the world." Crime would certainly exist in the United States even if gun ownership were controlled as tightly as in Japan, for instance. But the ready availability of the lethal and conceal-able handgun facilitates street and shop robberies and turns what in many countries would be simple assaults into murders.

Critics of gun control contend that gun ownership can deter criminals. According to a recent poll by ABC News, many Americans must be buying this line—almost half of all households now have guns. But, as *Time* magazine reported in a 1981 special issue on crime, the chances are about six to one that a family's gun will end up injuring a family member and not a crook. And many family firearms that don't end up being used in a suicide, an accident or a dispute over use of the family car are stolen, for a total of more than 200,000 gun thefts each year.

There may also be an attitudinal factor behind high crime rates in the United States. While it is difficult to make cross-cultural comparisons, this country certainly stands out for its lively tradi-tion of glorifying its criminals, from Jesse James to *The Godfather*. In historian Joe B. Frantz's essay on the "frontier tradition" in *The History of Violence in America*, he cites a particularly outrageous example in the *Kansas City Times* of 1872. Three men on horses had ridden up to the entrance of the Kansas City Fair, shot at the ticket seller but missed him and hit a small girl in the leg. They then took off with something less than $1,000. As cruel and witless as this heist was, it nonetheless inspired one John N. Edwards of the *Times* to write with unabashed admiration that the robbery was "so diabolically daring and so utterly in contempt of fear that we are bound to admire it and revere its perpetrators."

Other criminals of the West were lionized because they were, like the James brothers, former Confederate raiders whose lawlessness could be seen by uncritical sympathizers as a carrying on of the South's cause. The fact that the targets of western "social bandits" were often banks and railroads, neither of which were beloved by frontier farmers or ranchers, added to the gunmen's appeal.

This tradition flourished again in the 1920s and 1930s. ABC-TV commentator Hughes Rudd caught the flavor of growing up at a time when thugs like Pretty Boy Floyd and Machine Gun Kelly were on the scene: "Since most of those characters were robbing banks, which we assumed had all the money we didn't have, we thought of them as sort of modern-day Robin Hoods in wide-brim fedoras and two-tone black and white shoes. Not heroes, exactly. Not somebody you'd want to take home to meet your sister but pretty daring fellows nonetheless. Now what on earth was the matter with us in those days?"

The baby boom and crime

The question "Why America?" has few easy answers; the question "Why now?" has some.

For a number of reasons, the United States between about 1930 and 1960 experienced an era of relatively little violence, criminal or otherwise. In retrospect, it is apparent that the country was benefiting from some demographic good fortune—the proportion of the U.S. population in the fourteen- to twenty-four age group that is most responsible for crime stayed relatively low throughout that period. That pattern changed, however, in the 1960s as the children of the postwar baby boom began showing up in the nation's high schools and its juvenile courts.

Silberman calls it "demographic overload." Between 1960 and 1970, the number of fourteen- to twenty-four-year-olds grew by more than 50 percent, with the ratio of youths to adults increasing by 39 percent. It was, as Silberman points out, the first time that ratio had increased in seventy years. The always difficult task that a society faces of taking young people and teaching them the society's shared values and goals was greatly complicated by these numbers. There were proportionately fewer adults to do the job and proportionately more young people to resist assimilation and to develop a youth counterculture that helped to delay the acceptance of the discipline, industry and self-denial associated with maturity. In any case, the rate of increase in crime substantially exceeded what would have been the rise if the growing numbers of young people had committed crimes at the same rate as their predecessors. They substantially surpassed those rates, and the crime boom of the 1960s and 1970s was on.

The demographic bulge was worldwide and goes a long way toward explaining why the rise of crime in this country was mirrored by increases in western Europe and elsewhere. By the same census-taker's token, the fall in the birth rate at the end of the 1960s is probably responsible for much of the recent decline in U.S. crime rates. Interestingly, average Scholastic Aptitude Test results of college-bound U.S. students reversed their traditional climb upward and began declining in the mid-1960s as the crime surge began to speed up and now, as the population of seventeen- and eighteen-year-olds declines (and crime incidence drops), those SAT scores are inching upward again. If criminologists are reluctant to put too much reliance on population trends as an answer to crime problems, it is because birth rates in the population groups most likely to commit crimes have not fallen as dramatically as they have for the nation as a whole.

As gloomy as the chronicle of criminal violence in this country is, there are constructive lessons to be learned from it. The pattern has been that certain forms of crime or violence enjoy a heyday of greater or lesser duration and then either vanish or become quite manageable problems. In some cases, all that is required is a solution as straightforward as the weapons-detection devices at airports that greatly reduced the spate of airplane hijackings that endangered air travel in the 1960s and early 1970s. Other forms of lawlessness, such as the vigilantism of the nineteenth century and early decades of this century, prove to be more persistent. But even nightriding finally gave way to stronger law enforcement by local government and a greater public tolerance for the kind of behavior deemed punishable by the vigilantes.

Labor violence provides an interesting case. While it still reappears from time to time, its incidence was greatly reduced by the passage of the National Labor Relations Act, also known as the Wagner Act, in 1935. By legitimizing collective bargaining by workers and by providing a federal mechanism for refereeing labor disputes, the New Deal congressmen who passed that law defused the bitter organizing struggles that had been taking lives for decades.

During that same decade, Congress and the states also repealed Prohibition. That was another case of a simple political act having a profound effect on the level of criminal violence. Many of the bootlegging gangs remained intact and branched into other areas after repeal, but the end of Prohibition certainly reduced the hijackings, gang shootouts and police corruption that were part and parcel of the "noble experiment." Needless to say, repeal also meant that the millions of Americans who had never given up alcohol also ceased their lawbreaking.

Race riots have marred the American scene for such a long time and under such differing circumstances (in the earlier incidents, blacks were almost always more the focus of riots than instigators of riots) that it would be foolhardy to say that the nation will never again experience the wave of burning, looting and destruction that broke out in the 1960s. Disturbances in recent years in Miami indicate that, in some cities at least, all the conditions still exist for renewed rioting.

In other cities, however, great changes have come since the 1960s. While the police force of Detroit in 1967 was only 5.6 percent black, that figure rose by 1983 to 31.6 percent. In other cities, the pattern has been the same. Incidents still occur in which white policemen use what blacks consider to be undue force in law-enforcement situations, but these often heated disagreements have been less likely in recent years to mushroom into civil disturbances.

The much more active role that blacks have played in the political affairs of large U.S. cities has also certainly diminished the 1960s resentment that the power structure was totally at odds with cities' minority-group residents. In 1983, there are black mayors in Detroit, Newark, Los Angeles, Hartford, Atlanta and Gary. One of the problems of the 1980s facing all big-city mayors, black or white, will be to maintain the gains made in integrating police forces and other city departments in the face of extreme budgetary pressure. The country will be neglecting hard-earned lessons of the 1960s if it lets tight budgets and last-hired, first-fired layoff policies reverse the progress made in bringing minority-group citizens into municipal departments—especially the uniformed ones.

The history of violence and lawbreaking in the United States offers some hope, then, that changes in society or its laws can lead to decided improvements. When Americans develop over time a balanced, rational consensus on what needs to be done, they can overcome inertia and do it. Achieving such a consensus on the problem of crime will be a great deal easier, however, if the national debate on the subject is stripped of a lot of its red herrings and myths.

condemned Bowery building

Chapter 2

Americans on edge

In Hingham a couple of weeks ago, a twelve-year-old
boy got lost on his way home from a friend's house. It
was dusk and he was walking in an unfamiliar
neighborhood. He knocked on four different doors
and nobody would let him in to make a phone call.
When his mother finally found him and returned
angrily to the houses to ask people why they wouldn't
let a twelve-year-old use the phone, she was asked,
"Don't you read the papers?"

The Boston Globe, *March 18, 1983*

n addition to the deaths, injuries
and financial losses that individuals have suffered at the hands of
criminals, crime has done something else to life in the United
States. It has made us less open, less trusting. To the extent that
these qualities have always struck visitors to the continent as
being typical of North Americans, crime has made us less
American.

Ten or fifteen years ago, a lost twelve-year-old wandering through a
prosperous bedroom community like Hingham, Massachusetts,
would not have had four doors closed in his face. A December
1982 ABC-News poll on attitudes toward crime revealed that 85
percent of the population always lock their doors when they go
out. Two decades ago, this wasn't the case. According to the poll, of
those in the sample who had their own houses or apartments
twenty years ago, 53 percent said that back then they locked their
doors less frequently than they do now.

Crime has made us fearful. Eighty-four percent of those questioned in the ABC poll thought that the crime rate was rising, even
though—according to FBI figures—it is slightly declining. When
the public was asked what national problems justify the expend-
iture of more federal money, only unemployment rated a higher
priority than crime, for which 75 percent advocated more outlays.

To a certain extent, the fear and concern about crime uncovered
in the ABC poll are constructive. Basic security precautions—
such as locking house and car doors—are sensible measures.
Since the poll showed that a staggering 30 percent of all city
dwellers were victims of some form of crime (mostly property
crime) last year, a healthy fear of criminals is hardly irrational
among city residents, especially low-income ones who are criminals' most frequent victims. If fear of crime also helps state
officials raise the money needed to build enough prison cells to
house overcrowded inmate populations in humane conditions
with better opportunities for rehabilitation, so much the better,
although officials who play up to this fear are going to have to
contend with a disappointed public if the construction of new
prison space does *not* reduce the crime rate.

But the fear of crime turns harmful when it becomes so ingrained
in the nation's public life that it distorts political debate, weakens
support for basic civil liberties or leads to ill-considered "solutions" to the crime problem that create as many difficulties as they
solve. An example of how crime can distort politics is its frequent
injection into campaigns for offices that have little or nothing to
do with the criminal-justice system. The 1977 race for mayor in
New York City turned, in part, on the so-called issue of capital
punishment, notwithstanding the fact that mayors have no voice
in the establishment of penalties for felony crimes. Repeatedly,
crime or "law and order" has been an issue in presidential campaigns, even though federal attorneys and federal courts deal with
only a very limited realm of crime and, with the exception of drug-
law enforcement and the occasional appeal to the federal courts of
a constitutional issue, have virtually nothing to do with the street
crimes that are of such concern to the public.

The fear of crime can be damaging in another way as well if it
drives so many law-abiding city residents off the streets that
unwary pedestrians lack the safety in numbers that a bustling
neighborhood provides. The police director of Newark, New Jersey,
Hubert Williams, discussed this phenomenon in a February 1983
discussion with ABC News. "It is important," he said, "to deal with
the problem of fear because fear is related to crime in a variety of

ways. For example, the more people that you have that are concerned in the streets, the more public visibility of people going about their normal lives, I believe, effects a reduction in crime through deterrence... If you have large groups of citizens in the street going about their lives, it constitutes a protection."

George Kelling of the Harvard Law School, in an interview with ABC News in early 1983, referred to recent research that indicated that much of the public's fear of crime is actually fear of disorder—public drunkenness, panhandling and rude behavior. This, he said, helps to explain why levels of fear are often higher in areas with relatively little crime than in areas with more crime but less disorder. Kelling is a strong advocate of high police visibility to help control that disorder and, consequently, fear. "When citizens feel that police are around," he said, "citizens themselves are more likely to intervene on their own behalf when they feel intimidated or threatened or something's going on." This willingness of citizens themselves to do things to "maintain social control on the streets" is crucial in controlling crime, Kelling believes. The technique of fighting crime by easing the public's fear of it is by no means a simple one: A Massachusetts police officer involved in crime prevention warns against the "false sense of security" that some anti-crime programs can instill. But if, as many criminologists believe, a high rate of crime in a city or neighborhood reflects a breakdown in traditional community controls, a first step in reconstructing those controls will require getting over the hurdle of fear that keeps solid citizens behind locked doors and leaves streets to criminals and risk-takers.

***Do the media
misreport crime?***

At what point does the public's fear of crime cross the line from constructive concern to self-defeating hysteria? It's a tricky question, but the ABC-News poll offered some insights. While a whopping 84 percent of the public did think, incorrectly, that crime is on the increase nationally, those surveyed showed a surer knowledge of what is happening to crime levels in their own communities. Fully 73 percent said that violent crime in their own neighborhood was either going down (22 percent) or staying about the same (51 percent). Only 24 percent said it was rising. This may just reflect the oft-observed feeling of safety that familiar surroundings impart—even when those surroundings are actually highly unsafe. But the results also reflect the reality: For most American communities, the crime rate is stabilizing or falling. The public responded in a similar vein when those polled in the survey were asked whether they felt safe walking alone at night on their neighborhood streets—79 percent said yes.

To the extent that crime does have the public slightly buffaloed, it is more in the public's perception of crime as a general problem for society than in a person's own neighborhood. The media, print and broadcasting, may bear a measure of responsibility for the public's sense that crime is engulfing society. Newspapers and radio and television stations often give more coverage to one violent crime than they do to the annual FBI report on the overall incidence of crime in society. Moreover, coverage of that FBI report is rarely detailed enough to point out, for instance, that 55 percent of all murders are committed by relatives or acquaintances of the victims. Nor do many news accounts of the FBI statistics make it clear that of the 13.3 million crimes tabulated by the FBI, fully 90 percent are crimes against property, such as burglary, and not crimes against the person.

The media's coverage of crime also distorts reality by focusing on the occasional violent attacks on middle-class residents of a city, while largely ignoring the far more common violent incidents in cities' low-income neighborhoods. Rarely do the media make it clear that blacks are two and a half times as likely to be the victims of crimes as whites are.

In a February 1983 panel discussion of crime and how it is affected by the media, the president of the Police Foundation, Patrick Murphy, said he was more concerned about television's handling of crime in its news reports than in its entertainment programs. In his travels about the country, he said, he has seen crime news handled differently in different places. When it is "sensationalized," he said, "people get more emotional and they don't address the real issues of how we can solve this crime problem."

Murphy is not alone in his criticism. During an ABC-News "Viewpoint" broadcast in February 1983 that looked at several sides of the relationship between the media and violence, television was taken to task by Rudolph Giuliani, who was then serving as associate U.S. attorney general. Accusing TV of "overdramatizing and oversimplifying" crime news, he faulted the medium's coverage in this area and said it handled developments in the economy or in foreign policy in a more sophisticated way. TV presents crime in "almost an entertainment way," Giuliani said, "rather than getting into the issues and the contending viewpoints on what causes crime, what can be done about the problems of crime. And I think in that sense you really create a very, very unrealistic picture of violence and crime in America." The medium was defended, to a degree, during the broadcast by John Corporon, senior vice president of WPIX-TV News in New York. Corporon conceded that there were excesses in this area, admitting that "some news executives display abhorrent thought processes" and "appear to be almost mindless on the subject." But he said he thought stations were being more responsible in this area than they were five or ten years ago.

Proving an actual causal link between the media's treatment of crime and any of the various wise or unwise crime-fighting steps that legislatures have taken is no easy matter. In its way, it is as difficult as proving a causal link between entertainment violence on television and aggressive behavior in children or adults. But a professor at the Harvard Law School, Alan Dershowitz, is quite certain that the public's fears are having an effect, sometimes an undesirable one, on the nation's criminal-justice system. "The frightened public," he told ABC News in an interview in early 1983, "creates a frightened judiciary which often—particularly if they are elected—is really afraid to do justice. And it does create a situation where we're all hostage to fear." Dershowitz blames politicians as well as the media for feeding this emotion. His own concern is that this fear could "realistically lead toward repression."

Politicians distort the crime issue both during campaigns and after they have taken office. Whenever new proposals are being presented there is a tendency to justify the expenditures asked for them by exaggerating the dimensions of the problem they are supposed to solve. An example of this was in March of 1983, when President Reagan came up with a new package of anticrime proposals (few of which would affect in any direct way crime in the streets). As the legislation was being unveiled, an aide of the president told the press, "The goal is to roll back the rising tide of crime." In fact, of course, the tide is not rising, but no politician wants to admit that his crime policy is going to have less effect on this serious national problem than broad demographic patterns have.

A nation with
several crime rates
At bottom, the question is not whether or not Americans are overly fearful of crime but whether that fear is being felt by those who should feel it and whether it is being put to constructive purposes. Indeed, one might argue that, in certain parts of the population, there is not enough fear of crime. Professor Franklin E. Zimring of the University of Chicago points out that levels of measured fear about crime among young black males are relatively low, even though they are the most likely victims of violent crime—as well as the most likely perpetrators of it. "The problem with citizen fear of crime in the suburbs and the safer sections of the city is that it's so undifferentiated," said Zimring in an interview with ABC News. "You can't say there's too much fear. You can't say there's too little. You can say the wrong people fear the wrong crimes."

For criminologist Norval Morris, also of the University of Chicago, crime occurs in different parts of the country at such different rates that "there really isn't an American crime rate." For most of the country, he said in an interview with ABC News in early 1983, there are, by international standards, "fairly ordinary crime rates," although homicide rates, for reasons peculiar to our society, are higher. Otherwise, and with the exception of what he calls "terribly destroyed pockets" in U.S. cities, the crime situation in this country is not much different from what it is in western Europe and the rest of the world. "A crime rate," said Morris, "for a state or country is putting together very different figures, then averaging, which doesn't give a very good perspective."

His point is well taken in connection with Hingham, Massachusetts. In 1981, that town of 20,440 reported no homicides, three rapes, fourteen robberies and eleven aggravated assaults. Its assault rate was less than one-fourth the national average, its robbery rate less than one-third and its rape rate less than one-half. There *is* crime in Hingham: Its 294 burglaries in 1981 ranked only slightly less than the U.S. average. But it's not the kind of crime that would make homeowners consider it an unacceptable risk to let a lost twelve-year-old use the telephone. It was fear that did that.

prison
hallway

Chapter 3

The perpetrators

As part of a seventeen-year study, what has
impressed me in our findings is not the environment
but how people perceive and react to that
environment. Crime is a product of the way that
people think. Criminals have a very different world
view, well captured in the statement of one man who
said, "When I walk into a house everything in that
room belongs to me." These are people who have
made choices from a very early age to take a path
different from most of their responsible brothers,
sisters and neighbors.

*—Stanton Samenow, a clinical psychologist
and co-author of* The Criminal Personality

In 1981, the police in the United
States made 2,420,800 arrests for the offenses that get totaled up on
the FBI Index—murder, rape, robbery, aggravated assault, burglary,
larceny, arson. While many crime statistics are likely to be affected
by various forms of overreporting or nonreporting, the arrest
figures for the Index crimes are fairly solid. Unless otherwise speci-
fied, any mention of crimes in this chapter refers to Index crimes.

For many years, criminologists believed that they could not get
a genuinely representative view of criminals by focusing their
studies on those who were arrested. The fact of their arrest, it was
assumed, meant they were the less gifted, less successful of the
breed. In recent years, that view has changed. While there undoubtedly are individuals who commit very few crimes, elude capture
and then go straight, interviews with offenders have established
fairly clearly that virtually everyone who commits crimes regularly

is going to get caught at one time or another. The arrest statistics are thus a reliable source of information about the criminals who have Americans so frightened.

Men's work

Those FBI-compiled data from more than 15,000 jurisdictions around the country present a fairly clear profile of the criminal, who is, by all means, a he. Males accounted for 81 percent of arrests, 90 percent of those for violent crimes, 79 percent of those for property-crime offenses. But while women are still greatly outnumbered by men in this field, between 1972 and 1981 female arrests rose at an even higher rate (61 percent) than male (51 percent). In a few areas in particular, such as burglary, larceny and motor-vehicle theft, the increases over ten years in female arrests have been especially dramatic. In certain non-Index crimes, such as fraud, the figure for female arrests in 1981 (100,740) comes close to the male figure (140,447). Still, when it comes to the kinds of crime that are of most immediate concern to the public, women are much less likely than men to be the perpetrators.

The average criminal is also young. No fewer than 67 percent of all those arrested in 1981 were under twenty-five; 51 percent were under twenty-one. Eighteen-year-olds in 1981 committed more robberies than criminals of any other age; nineteen-year-olds more murders. But the fall-off in birth rates from the late 1960s and 1970s is beginning to be felt in crime statistics. Since 1977, the number of males under eighteen years of age who were arrested fell by 9 percent; the number of females by 12 percent.

Just as the victims of crimes are disproportionately likely to be members of minority groups, so are the perpetrators. Blacks, who make up about 12 percent of the population, account for 34 percent of all arrests. For violent crimes alone, the black percentage is even higher: 45.7. Hispanic Americans account for 10.4 percent of arrests (11.8 percent of violent-crime arrests), a portion somewhat higher than their representation in the population (6.5 percent), but the per-capita arrest rate of Hispanic Americans is not as high as blacks'.

The FBI data also provide a clear picture of where most crime is committed—in cities. In 1981, the rate of robberies was 322 per 100,000 population in large metropolitan areas; more than 60 per 100,000 in other, smaller cities; and fewer than 21 in rural counties. This pattern holds right down the line for property crimes. The one divergence from it is for murder: Murder rates are somewhat higher in rural counties than they are in small cities.

The above figures on the sex, age and race or ethnic group of criminals give us a rough picture of American criminals and where they operate, but they don't say much about what happened in their lives before they became statistics in the FBI Uniform Crime Report. Periodically, criminologists or just plain poll-takers have gone into jails or prisons to interview inmates to get a better view of their backgrounds. One such survey was done in 1982 by the *Washington Post* at Lorton, a Washington, D.C., correctional facility. Imprisoned offenders tend to have longer records than "typical" criminals and the inmate population at Lorton is both more urban than the national average and made up disproportionately of blacks. But the results probably give a fairly typical picture of the life histories of street criminals.

According to the *Post* survey, 51 percent of the inmates said their parents were divorced or separated; 35 percent said their families had to "worry about where the next meal was coming from"; 54 percent reported that some other member or members of their families had served time in jail or prison; and 38 percent agreed that "many of the older people I looked up to were involved in drugs or crime." Only 35 percent said they were not involved in crime before the age of eighteen; the median age of inmates' first incarceration was sixteen. Almost two-thirds of the inmates said they had used marijuana in the past; 43 percent said they had used other illegal drugs; and 33 percent said they had been addicted to drugs. But asked to give the "main reason" that got them "into trouble," 65 percent said it was the desire to secure money for "day to day living," not to support a drug habit or get money for "a car and nice clothes."

The worst 10 percent

Other researchers have done inmate surveys and interviews not to explore the causes of crime but to devise strategies aimed at identifying—and the earlier the better—those criminals who commit the most crimes. One such study was done by Jan M. Chaiken, a senior mathematician at the Rand Corporation, and Marcia R. Chaiken, a UCLA sociologist. They took a close look at 2,200 inmates in jails and prisons in Texas, California and Michigan and, using confidential reports from the inmates, singled out what they called "the violent predators," offenders who had committed robbery, assaults and drug offenses—at the minimum. The worst 10 percent of these violent predators committed crimes of all these kinds (and often burglary, as well) at much higher rates than other inmates who were "just" robbers or "just" assaulters.

A composite of the Chaikens' "worst 10 percent" criminal is a young man who has been committing crimes, especially violent ones, since before the age of sixteen. These criminals usually have spent time in juvenile correctional institutions and are, generally, "more socially unstable" than other inmates. They are less likely to be married or have family obligations and have, at best, checkered employment records. Most, reported the Chaikens, began using "hard" drugs early, while still juveniles, and then moved on to heavy use of a wide variety of substances, including alcohol, barbiturates, amphetamines and heroin.

By some estimates, these "worst 10 percent" criminals commit almost one half of all the serious crime in this country. Many criminologists and some officials in the criminal-justice system believe that identifying these "career criminals" and making certain they receive, and serve, lengthy sentences would be a particularly effective anticrime step. But the Chaikens point out that this technique, which will be discussed in more detail later in this book, has at least one hitch: Because the career criminals are often so young, their adult arrest records rarely show enough offenses to justify the "worst 10 percent" designation. And it goes without saying that they are unlikely to report such offenses, as they might on a confidential basis for researchers, if they know that their length of sentence or chance of parole will be affected. Juvenile arrest records might help in the selection process, but their availability is very catch-as-catch-can. Partly because of confidentiality rules and, in some cases, because of "bureaucratic sloth," to use the Chaikens' phrase, juvenile records are often not seen by judges or prosecutors.

The pattern of a relatively small group of offenders committing disproportionate amounts of crime that shows up in the Chaikens' work was evident in a 1973 study done at the University of Pennsylvania by Marvin E. Wolfgang, Robert Figlio and Thorsten Sellin. Those researchers looked at the delinquency records of every boy who was born in Philadelphia in 1945 and lived there between the ages of ten and eighteen, a group of almost 10,000 in all. Not all, of course, accumulated juvenile or adult records, but a noteworthy percentage did. Fully 35 percent had, by the age of eighteen, a run-in with the police for something more serious than a traffic violation. By the age of twenty-six, 43 percent had been arrested as either a juvenile or an adult.

As alarming as that high incidence of delinquent behavior is, other data in the Wolfgang study help to put it in perspective. Of the 35 percent who were brought in as delinquents, almost half committed just one offense and often these offenses were not, in an adult sense, criminal. They were truants from school or runaways from home. The one-time offenders accounted for just a tiny fraction of all the serious crimes committed by those born in 1945.

Of far more concern to Philadelphia's law-enforcement system were the 1,862 boys who were collared more than once. They committed 90 percent of the sample's total crimes. But the most serious lawbreakers were those, numbering 627, who were arrested five times or more. Although they constituted less than one-fifth of the delinquent group of 3,500, they were responsible for half of all the crimes and for about two-thirds of the violent crimes.

Subsequently, Wolfgang and associates studied a larger "cohort" of 28,000 Philadelphia boys born in 1958. The same patterns, with some unsettling variations, emerged. The percentage of repeat offenders rose from the 6 percent of the 1945-born group to 7.5 percent. Of particular concern is that the overall rate of serious offenses among the 1958 cohort rose by an alarming 69 percent. Overall, their violent-crime rate was three times as high as that recorded by the 1945 contingent. Wolfgang has said, in summary, that the youths born in 1958 include "a very violent criminal population of a small number of nasty brutal offenders."

An interesting though hardly surprising pattern that became clear in Wolfgang's study of Philadelphia's 1945-born males was the statistical link between certain socioeconomic factors and a youth's high arrest rate. The researchers discovered that one-time juvenile delinquents did not differ much from nondelinquents in their economic class, their IQs or their performance in school. This was not the case, though, when the one-time delinquents and the nondelinquents were compared with the multiple offenders. The latter were much more likely to be from a lower social class, to have lower IQs, to do poorly in school and to come from a broken home.

*Frustrating search
for causes*

In the jargon of criminologists, factors in a person's background like poverty, failure in school and a disrupted home life are not, as such, causes of crime, although they may "correlate strongly" with criminal behavior. The "cause" of crime is a kind of Holy Grail for a wide range of academic disciplines, from psychology to nutrition. But the search for a key to violent or deviant behavior that could, for instance, explain why one boy brought up in a low-income, broken home turns out to be a model citizen and his brother becomes a thief has not been very productive. One specialist in the field, Norval Morris of the University of Chicago, once went so far as to propose, only half in jest, a flat prohibition on research into the causes of crime, although he would wholeheartedly support thorough research evaluating the effects of crime prevention and control programs.

Morris, in his book, *The Honest Politician's Guide to Crime Control*, relates an anecdote that suggests some of the complexity of the seemingly straightforward question, what causes crime? While serving in Asia in the early 1960s as a director of a United Nations institute for crime prevention, Morris was asked by trainees from relatively undeveloped Asian countries with traditionally low deliquency rates how they might head off the deliquency problems that seemed to be growing more common. The trainees must have been taken aback when Morris told them that the problem could be nipped in the bud if they would ensure that their people remained "ignorant, bigoted and ill-educated." Industrial growth he said, should be blocked; communications systems must remain primitive; and transportation development should be discouraged so that the people lived out their entire lives in their small villages. Under no circumstances must children ever get it into their heads that they could rise to a station higher than their father's or, he told the trainees, "the seed of the gravest disorder would be laid."

In the United States, for better or for worse, the seeds of disorder have not only long since been laid but have germinated and grown into a riotously profuse maturity. There is no getting around the point that Morris makes: Crime seems linked almost inextricably with the tensions, frustrations and temptations of an open and mobile society that places a high value on individual development at the expense of the family or community.

But what makes many students of the subject dissatisfied with the notion that crime ultimately stems from basically unknowable (or unreachable) roots that cannot successfully be attacked by a government of limited powers is the great difference that exists between the severity of the U.S. crime problem and that of a country like Canada or Great Britain. As sociologist Elliott Currie points out, even granting the truth of Harvard Professor James Q. Wilson's statement on the imperfectibility of man, "Wicked people exist," there have to be reasons why so many more of them ply their wickedness in the United States than in countries like Britain or Japan. Nor can the answer lie simply in some peculiarly American bad gene or a fatal flaw in the U.S. criminal-justice system. The difference between the murder rate of California (13 per 100,000 in 1981) and Minnesota (2.1 per 100,000) is substantially larger than the difference between the overall U.S. rate and that of less violent industrialized countries, like Japan.

If Japan has, to date at least, largely escaped crime problems on a Western scale, it may be, as Ezra Vogel suggests in *Japan as Number 1*, because modern Japanese society has managed to keep intact some of the traditions of family and community identification and responsibility that appear to deter aberrant behavior. Vogel points out that a school principal or teacher in Japan is considered so responsible for the behavior of his students that when one gets in touble with the police, the principal or teacher may be asked to resign or "at least apologize publicly."

That feeling of group responsibility is virtually unknown in the United States. But another sharp difference between growing up in Japan and growing up in the United States is the high level of unemployment in the former. Japan considers it a national crisis when, as in the recent worldwide slump, its unemployment rate exceeds 2 percent.

The belief that high crime rates are strongly related to high unemployment rates is held by a substantial majority of the public. When the ABC-News poll asked, "What would you say is most responsible for this country's high crime rate?" the answer was quite emphatic. Fifty-eight percent attributed it to "unemployment, poverty and the like." No other factor—not drugs (18 percent), not "breakdown of family, society, moral values" (15 percent), not "courts too lenient" (12 percent)—came even close. In light of all the statistics that have been compiled demonstrating the "strong correlation" between poverty and crime, this is a sound and perfectly understandable answer to the question.

*Crime waves
amid prosperity*
By the late 1960s and early 1970s, however, this explanation of the cause of crime had begun to come under fire. The 1960s were a time of rapidly expanding economic opportunities for Americans, yet crime during this decade was rising at a precipitous rate. Actually, the paradox is not all that difficult to explain. There are a number of reasons why crime rates rose during this period, the most important of which is the "demographic overload" that was referred to in Chapter 1. For all the overall prosperity of the decade, neither the schools nor the employers of the nation were prepared to handle the sudden upsurge in young people. In 1950, 34 per cent of the vacant jobs could be filled by someone with less than a high school diploma. By 1970, when the baby-boom generation was flooding the job market, that figure had fallen to 8 percent. Even a criminologist like James Q. Wilson, who puts little stock in fighting crime by going to its "root causes," points out in his book *Thinking About Crime* that in Washington, D.C., the unemployment rate for blacks aged sixteeen to twenty-one had remained steadily around 8 per-

cent during the 1950s and then shot up to 16 percent for males and 20 percent for females by 1970. There *were* years during the 1960s when the unemployment rate of black male teenagers subsided slightly, but between 1955 and 1971, that rate more than doubled, rising from 13.4 percent to 28.8 percent. M. Harvey Brenner of Johns Hopkins University, who has made a study of the social consequences of youth unemployment, came to several conclusions, one of which was that the social pathology of youth unemployment is related not so much to the overall unemployment rate but, rather, to the discrepancy between the youth unemployment rate and that overall figure. The 1960s may have been a time of declining overall unemployment in the United States, but it was a time when, in the nation's largest cities, the numbers of unemployed youths rose substantially.

What governments can do well

The objection that Harvard's Wilson and others raise to fighting crime by getting at underlying conditions like youth unemployment is not that the two problems are unrelated but, rather, that government just isn't very good at this kind of intervention. Moreover, he and others contend, focusing on the socioeconomic causes of crime is often a liberal's way of neglecting other proposals to make the criminal-justice system more effective by raising the likelihood that criminals will go to prison and serve long sentences there. The demand for causal solutions is, Wilson wrote in *Thinking About Crime*, "whether intended or not, a way of deferring any action and criticizing any policy. It is a cast of mind that inevitably detracts attention from those few things that governments can do reasonably well and draws attention toward those many things it cannot do at all."

Wilson's book, which was first published in 1975, and other writings by him and criminologists of similar views became the guiding spirit for most of society's new approaches to crime-fighting in the 1970s and even into the 1980s. Wilson, in fact, served on the Attorney General's Task Force on Violent Crime that was established by the Reagan administration in 1981. The task force report directly reflects the views of *Thinking About Crime*: "The causes of crime are variously said to be found in the weakening of familial and communal bonds, the persistence of unacceptable social disadvantages among some segments of society and the easy spread of attitudes that favor immediate over deferred gratification." But, the report's authors say, the task force chose not to pursue these matters for several reasons. Among them was the members' lack of conviction that "a government, by the invention of new programs or the management of existing institutions, can by itself re-create those familial and neighborhood conditions, those social opportunities and those personal values that in all likelihood are the prerequisites of tranquil communities." It is, to say the least, an unmincing statement of the laissez-faire view that government has few arrows in its quiver when it goes about attacking this social problem that is of such intense concern to so much of the public.

The differing views of what society can and cannot do in this area were spelled out during an ABC panel discussion aired in February of 1983. The three principal participants were criminologist Marvin Wolfgang, Stanton Samenow, a clinical psychologist and co-author of a book called *The Criminal Personality*, and Patrick Murphy, the former New York City police commissioner who is president of the Police Foundation. Samenow took the stance that exploring the causes of crime offers little hope for handling it better: "We've been mired in theories about causes for years. We looked at social backgrounds, some possible physical factors, psychological factors. We had to leave cause on the shelf and say we simply don't know at this point. But we've got to deal with the person and his thinking and to understand how these people think. Where does it all come from? It's like many other conditions, we simply don't know. But we can't continue to base our policies on causative theories."

Wolfgang agreed that "poverty is not necessarily associated with crime because there are many poor and law-abiding people." But, he said, "in America we have a long tradition of blacks who have been subjugated, disadvantaged, ill-educated and ill-housed and ill-fed in many ways, and those socioeconomic variables are clearly associated with crime." Murphy, the former policeman, saw little hope of containing crime without addressing its socioeconomic background. "We have to understand that you can't keep cramming all of our poor people into the cities and have the middle class fleeing to the suburbs and find solutions. When that happens, state governments and the federal government have to help the cities, not only with crime control but with social and economic programs," he said.

In any case, the parameters of the debate have certainly shifted over the past fifteen years. It is difficult to find many liberals in 1983 who would not support more funding for effective local police programs or better-staffed courts and prosecutors' offices in the criminal-justice mills of the big cities. On the other hand, even many of those criminologists who place little value in looking at the causes of crime argue, nonetheless, that society should do its best to ameliorate the poverty, unemployment, poor education and bad housing that go hand in hand with crime simply because that is the decent thing to do. "We wish," writes Norval Morris in *The Honest Politician's Guide to Crime Control,* "to get rid of slums, not particularly because they are productive of delinquency and crime but because we think they are a despicable way for people to have to live. We wish to facilitate happy and stable family lives not because we wish to reduce delinquency but because, all in all, we think that is the better way for people to live."

Unfortunately, in the United States no consensus exists for devoting enough public resources to improve the living conditions of the poor and ill educated. This debate on how best to attack crime is important precisely because the resources for correcting any social problem are limited. Whatever approach is taken to fighting crime will, inevitably, involve the use of federal and state funds. How those funds are spent—whether for more police, more prosecutors, more prisons or more youth-unemployment programs or child-care facilities—will necessarily involve public officials' perceptions of, if not the causes of crime, the best ways to prevent and control it.

The tendency to fight crime with such limited programs was lamented by criminologist Franklin E. Zimring of the University of Chicago. "When a budget that is addressed to the problem of crime is to be divided up," he said in an ABC-News interview, "it is divided up amongst the usual suspects. Sure, experiments will fail, sure a lot of what during the seventies went for community involvement was a WPA program for the employees. But you can't even get to the worthwhile experiment until the public-policy perception of what can be done in relation to crime is broader than the existing agencies of the criminal-justice system."

So the question is at least worth posing: Would a concerted effort to put more resources into the education of the disadvantaged young and into youth-employment programs be a worthwhile government initiative for purposes of crime prevention, not to mention the other ends that such programs could achieve?

As for the education of the culturally deprived, Washington already is making some special efforts in this area, although debate continues over whether they are sufficient. In addition to the Head Start program, the federal government has, since passage of the Elementary and Secondary Education Act of 1965, sent money for special instruction in the basic skills to school districts with large numbers of low-income students. Unfortunately, the program, Title 1 of the 1965 act, got off to a rocky start. Local school departments often diverted the funds from the purpose for which they were intended, and for several years it was impossible to trace any basic-skills gains to Title 1. In the early 1970s, however, the federal government cracked down in this area, tightening both its restrictions and its auditing. Since then, significant improvements have been registered. In 1981, the federally funded National Assessment of Education Progress reported that black nine-year-olds had increased their reading scores by 9 percentage points from 1971 to 1980. Other gains were reported for urban students, as a group, and for rural students.

The federal Department of Education has also given Chapter 1 (its name changed with passage of the Reagan administration's Education Consolidation and Improvement Act of 1981) a good report card. According to the department secretary's evaluation report of December 1981, Chapter 1 students in grades one through three improved in reading by 17 percent more than students of the same age who were not in the program. Even more dramatic gains were shown in mathematics for Chapter 1 students. Notwithstanding these successes, the Reagan administration in 1982 reduced funding for Chapter 1 and, for the fiscal 1984 budget, proposed converting the program to a voucher system. That would allow the parents of qualifying students to apply their children's share of Chapter 1 money to basic-skills programs outside of the public schools' curriculum. Critics of this proposal fear it might deprive public-school Chapter 1 programs of the basic support they need to continue to succeed in this area. The program nevertheless survives and apparently works. Supporters believe that with the infusion of more resources, it could significantly help reduce what many employers say is the biggest stumbling block to hiring the young: their inadequate mastery of basic skills.

The initial problems of 1965's Title 1 contributed to the widespread feeling common in the 1970s that many of the Great Society programs had fallen far short of their goals. This view also applies to the area of youth employment, where the Neighborhood Youth Corps of the 1960s was given little credit for anything more than "income maintenance." One Great Society employment program, the Job Corps, has won over many of its initial critics. With its combination of basic-skills and vocational instruction, it is considered by youth-employment experts to be the nation's most thorough and successful program in this area, despite the high cost per student. The 1970s were a period of both some success and much failure in youth employment. The jobs, especially summer jobs, financed by the Comprehensive Employment and Training Act did offer employment in some years to as many as two million Americans. But critics questioned whether many of the jobs were really doing much to develop a work ethic in the youngsters.

"We can't let the schools off the hook"

It was against this background of a mixed record in youth employment programs that James Q. Wilson, in 1975, wrote in *Thinking About Crime*: "We may be able to change the teenage unemployment rate, although we have learned by painful trial and error that doing this is much more difficult than once supposed." If anything, the eight years since he wrote that have shown just how difficult integrating teenagers into the work force can be, especially during a sustained slump like that of 1980–1983. In 1975, the teenage unemployment rate was slightly more than 20 percent. In the spring of 1983 it was about 30 percent; for black teenagers it was close to 50 percent.

But although Wilson puts his greatest emphasis on beefing up the law-enforcement system as a crime-prevention measure (the "things that governments can do reasonably well" in his phrase), he does not rule out altogether measures that open up greater opportunities for lawful behavior: "The benefits of work and the costs of crime must be increased simultaneously; to increase one without the other makes sense only if one assumes that young people are irrational."

Since Wilson wrote that, one of the most comprehensive efforts in this area came out of Vice President Walter Mondale's Task Force on Youth Employment during the Carter administration. Based on the work of that task force, President Carter proposed a two-part bill that, for the first time, would have linked the country's job-training programs with the public high schools in an attempt to get at the lack of educational and work skills that are keeping many young people out of the job market even in areas where overall unemployment is not severe. "Without assistance in obtaining basic skills," wrote psychologist Robert L. Green, dean of Michigan State's College of Urban Development, in 1980, "many young people will be unable to compete in the job market."

To a certain extent, the school component of the $2 billion 1980 bill would have done for junior-high and high-school students what Chapter 1 is already doing for elementary-school pupils: beefing up basic skills. But it would have combined this extra instruction in 3,000 schools serving low-income areas with preparation in work skills and with part-time, on-the-job training opportunities. For those out of school, the bill would have provided work experience, training and job counseling.

This pioneering legislation, part of which is reflected in 1982's Jobs Training Partnership Act, held out hope for getting at the difficult problems of functional illiteracy and unemployment among the young. It fell victim in 1980, however, to budget pressures and to reservations in the education community over the new role that the act would assign to secondary schools. In any case, it sits on the shelf as one blueprint for a problem that persists even in the event of a robust economic recovery. In 1981, Robert Shrank, who was then a program officer with the Ford Foundation, discussed this issue in a forum on youth unemployment in Boston: "Are there going to be enough jobs for all young people? I don't think so, because no matter how many jobs this economy develops—ten million jobs have been created in the last decade alone—they will attract more people into the labor market. This has a lot to do with the changing nature of work and the appeal of white-collar jobs. The fact of the matter is that an expanded labor market alone will not solve this problem. So what can we do? The real focus still has to be on the schools. . . . We cannot let the schools off the hook."

Elliott Currie, in two *Working Papers* articles in 1982, made another point in reference to studies that showed that crime is linked not just to employment or unemployment but to the quality of jobs that are available as well. "This suggests," he wrote, "that job quality and stability are the real issues Simply forcing the urban unemployed into new variants of low-wage, menial labor, as much current administration policy proposes, won't begin to come to grips with urban crime."

Could a consensus be built for new initiatives in this area to go along with the greater expenditures for the criminal-justice system? Currie believes that there are some grounds for optimism. He referred in his article to a recent Field Institute poll in California sponsored by the National Council on Crime and Delinquency which asked, "What will reduce crime in California?" It found that three fourths of those polled said that jobs would. Other crime-fighting proposals, such as building more prisons or adding to police forces, did not gain such a strong vote of confidence. These findings are not out of line with what ABC News found when 58 percent of the respondents in its poll listed unemployment and poverty as the major factors in crime. On this point, by the way, the nation has changed its views considerably over the years. A 1965 Gallup Poll on what the public thought lay behind crime increases indicated that more than half attributed the problem to faults in the moral character of the population. More objective conditions, such as unemployment, were mentioned by relatively few. In eighteen years, as both youth unemployment and crime rates have risen steeply, that view has changed. As Currie wrote: "If there is a way to cope with violent inner-city youth crime while the official jobless rate for black youth hovers around 40 percent, we have yet to hear what it is."

The American connection:
drugs and crime

A good example of how public officials' understanding of the causes of crime affects decisions on how crime-fighting money is spent is the federal government's current campaign to bring the illegal drug trade under control. In an ABC-News interview earlier this year, Attorney General William

French Smith left no doubt that he saw a link between crime and narcotics: "I think one thing stands out for sure, and that is that one of the princicpal known causes is drugs." And, in line with the recommendations of the 1981 task force, narcotics-control programs are a major part of Washington's crime-fighting efforts.

As it happens, however, experts in the field are as reluctant to describe drugs as a cause of crime as they are to blame crime on poverty alone. No one will deny that the trafficking in illegal narcotics is associated with a great deal of violence, just as the Prohibition-era bootlegging of alcohol was a violent business. But criminologists cannot find strong evidence to support the notion that many otherwise law-abiding individuals ever took to a life of crime *because* they were under the influence of, or needed money to buy, illegal drugs. A more common view is that narcotics are substances that, like alcohol, many but not all criminals use and, in some cases, abuse, much as a certain percentage of the country's solid citizens use and, in some cases, abuse both drugs and alcohol.

"Your typical robber is not somebody who's supporting anyone else," said Peter Greenwood, a criminologist with the Rand Corporation, in an interview with ABC News. "He's in it for himself and he sees it as a really fast life-style, and drugs are part of that lifestyle." Mark Moore, a Harvard University criminologist, made a similar point in an ABC-News interview: "I think it's very doubtful that all of the crimes committed by drug users should be attributed to their drug use in itself, which is to say that if they stopped using drugs tomorrow, they would still be committing a reasonable number of crimes."

A federal commission that studied the drug problem in the 1970s came to a similar conclusion. According to the National Commission on Marijuana and Drug Abuse, "criminal behavior is not a byproduct of dependence but results, as does the drug dependence itself, from psychological and social deviance which predates dependence." The commission made no bones about the fact that its conclusion on this point "challenges the theory that drugs cause crime and stresses that drug dependence and criminality are two forms of social deviance, neither producing the other."

None of this is meant to minimize the role of drugs in the life of criminals. The Lorton prison poll showed that 65 percent of the inmates had used at least marijuana before their arrest, 43 percent had used harder drugs and 33 percent described themselves as having been addicts. Nor did the fact of incarceration itself bring their use of drugs to an end. No fewer than 46 percent said they had used marijuana while serving time at Lorton. A convicted mugger from Brooklyn, Rufus Saunders, was asked in an interview with ABC News whether his use of cocaine and heroin had "pushed" him to commit crimes. "No," Saunders answered. "That was a lot of what was giving me the courage to do everything I wanted to. Okay? Heroin would give me the courage to say, 'I don't care what nobody thinks. I don't care what nobody feels. This is me and I'm going to do it my way. This is how I'm going to do it.'" The kind of "courage" that Saunders describes has also been known as "Dutch courage," boldness that comes out of the liquor bottle. One has the strong suspicion that if by some miracle illegal drugs were elim- inated from American society, criminals would simply rely more heavily for their kicks and their "cool" on abuse of the substance that has been part and parcel of the American crime problem throughout the nation's history—alcohol.

The other question that many experts raise is whether it is possible for law-enforcement agencies, including federal ones, to interdict effectively the supply of substances which, in the cases of marijuana and cocaine, are used by an estimated twenty-seven million Americans. As criminologist Andrew von Hirsch pointed out in an ABC-News interview: "Selling drugs is a good business. If you take a drug seller and lock him up, somebody else is likely to go into the same business." As for Washington's policy of applying pressure on foreign governments to cut off the supply of narcotics at its source, one federal narcotics official once pointed out that the entire heroin market can be supplied by just ten square miles of poppies "and they grow everywhere." Charles Silberman, in *Criminal Violence, Criminal Justice*, added to this the fact that it would take just two ten-ton trucks to bring a year's supply of heroin into the United States, and he estimates that in 1970 approx- imately sixty-five million cars and trucks crossed into this country.

Silberman's sober and balanced assessment of the chances of making major inroads into the crime problem by attacking the narcotics business is worth quoting: "It would be fatuous to suggest that the growth in heroin use has contributed nothing to the increase in crime; but we simply do not know how large that contribution is, or what the processes are through which drug abuse contributes to crime. Given the dimensions, as well as the complexity, of the drug abuse problem, no approach, be it decriminalization, tougher law enforcement, or new modes of treatment, can be counted on to bring about a major reduction in drug abuse or cime in the foreseeable future."

Much as Norval Morris believes that society should correct substandard social conditions, quite aside from their contribution to crime, drug abuse in the United States should also be dealt with as a problem in and of itself—and not just as an accompaniment or aggravator of crime. Dr. Richard Jessor, a social psychologist who is director of the Institute of Behavioral Science at the University of Colorado, said in a March 1983 interview with the *New York Times* that learning how to cope with drugs was becoming a standard stage in the development of the young. "It may now be a developmental task that young people need to come to terms with, like separation from parents, career development and sexuality," he said. "And so we ought to focus on education and provide the kinds of information and skills for the least irresponsible use of these substances." As difficult as that task will be, its effect may be more lasting than large federal investments in rabbit-and-hare chases of narcotics smugglers.

The troubled families of criminals

After unemployment and drugs, the aspect of modern society that respondents in the ABC-News poll found most blameworthy for the high incidence of crime was the "breakdown of family, society, moral values." The public's suspicion that these factors are closely tied to criminal behavior has a long tradition behind it. Three decades ago, sociologists Eleanor and Sheldon Glueck did pioneering work in isolating the conditions that seemed to predispose certain youths to become delinquents. On the basis of their data, they found that when other factors like age, neighborhood and intelligence were held constant, an important predictor of delinquency is the relative strength of the youth's family life—variables such as the family's stability and the degree and kind of parental affection and discipline.

More recent data make the same point. Elliott Currie observed in his July–August 1982 *Working Papers* article, "Fighting Crime," that in 1980, only 29 percent of the male wards and 19 percent of the female wards in the California Youth Authority came from "unbroken" families. In 1973, statistics showed that only 21 percent of the juveniles who came into New York City's family courts were from intact families. A Vera Institute study in the mid-1970s of juvenile offenders in New York State showed that just one third of them came from families in which both parents were alive and living together. Paul Strasburg, in *Violent Delinquents*, refers to a Massachusetts analysis of 700 children examined in court clinics. Of them, 46 percent of the children's parents were divorced or permanently separated; in 14 percent of the families one parent had died; 21.5 percent of the children had parents suffering from chronic illnesses; and 18 percent had parents who were severe alcoholics.

All of the evidence led University of Arizona professor Travis Hirschi to conclude, in an article published in the spring 1983 *Wilson Quarterly*, that, "In most, but not all, studies that directly compare children living with both biological parents and children living in a 'broken' or reconstituted home, the youngsters from intact families have lower rates of crime." Dr. Richard Rada, a clinical psychiatrist at the University of New Mexico and author of a book on rape, pointed out in an ABC-News interview in February 1983, that in studies of inmates who have committed violent crimes reveal "a large number who came from homes with violent backgrounds. You'd find a large number with parents who have also suffered from problems of alcoholism, particularly."

Currie, Strasburg and Hirschi are all quick to point out that, under the right circumstances, single-parent families can be just as successful as intact families in bringing up children of exemplary behavior. "Studies have shown," Strasburg writes, "that a single-parent home in which the child and parent have a good relationship may offer more protection against delinquency than a two-parent family in which relationships are strained." According to Currie, studies that have looked closely at the problems of single-parent families find that it is not the absence of one parent that causes difficulties so much as the lack "of enough outside resources, human and material, to insure an adequate developmental environment." Hirschi refers back to research by the Gluecks that indicated that in families in which the mother worked there was a higher rate of delinquency, but the mother's employment had no effect on the likelihood of delinquency when she "was able to provide supervision for her children."

If Currie is right, that insufficient resources are part of what makes many "broken" families so weak, the situation would seem to be deteriorating. Between 1971 and 1980, the number of families headed by a single female and living at or below the poverty level ($6,539 for a family of three in 1980) rose by 54 percent, from 2,100,000 to 3,245,000.

The connection between family violence and extremely violent children has emerged in sharp relief in research done by Dr. Dorothy O. Lewis, a professor of psychiatry at the New York University School of Medicine and Dr. Jonathan Pincus, a professor of neurology at Yale University School of Medicine. They studied twenty-one homicidally violent children between the ages of three and twelve who had been admitted to a psychiatric ward in New York City. Among these children, 62 percent had fathers who had been violent with their mothers, 50 percent had a history of psychomotor seizures and 57 percent had attempted to commit suicide. Thirty-seven percent of the fathers of the violent children had themselves been homicidally violent and 43 percent of their mothers had a history of psychiatric care in a hospital.

Dr. Lewis, Dr. Pincus and their colleagues also studied in 1979 seventy-eight juvenile delinquents. They found that violent offenders had been subjected in childhood to extreme levels of abuse. "Especially violent offenders," they reported, "have been victims of, and had witnessed, severe physical abuse."

In a 1982 interview with the *New York Times*, Dr. Pincus said that when he began to work in this area he did not expect to find that physiological factors were important in the background of violent youth, and the results of his own research surprised him. "But we know now," he said, "that there are three correlates that characterize the repeatedly violent child: neurological impairment, psychiatric symptoms and the history of having been abused. We're not certain they are the causative factors of violence, but we strongly suspect that this is so." Their research, Dr. Lewis points out, presents a strong argument for early treatment of such disturbed children. After a period of intensive treatment, she told the *Times*, the children will still need access to monitoring and ongoing treatment. Such treatment programs are now, she said, very limited.

Family-support systems

But while experts from both ends of the political spectrum may agree that poor parent-child relationships correlate strongly with crime, they quite emphatically disagree on the question of whether knowing this is any actual help in preventing crime. James Q. Wilson laments the fact that "disorganization is increasing" in families, but then goes on to write in *Thinking About Crime*: "If a child is delinquent because his family made him so or his friends encourage him to be so, it is hard to conceive what society might do about his attitudes. No one knows how a government might restore affection, stability and fair discipline to a family that rejects these characteristics; still less can one imagine how even a family once restored could affect a child who has passed the formative years and in any event has developed an aversion to one or both of his parents."

Currie takes sharp issue with this point of view. While he concedes that by the time delinquent youths come to the attention of the criminal-justice system their family problems may be beyond repair, he rejects the notion that U.S. society cannot do more for low-income families to make it easier for them to develop strong, nurturing relations between parents and children. For the long term, he proposes "changing the terms and conditions of women's work" and controlling "the forces that now so wantonly separate families from kin and friendship networks." For the short term, he favors "adequate income support for family heads who are unable to work" and development on a large scale of the supported-work programs for welfare mothers. "Changing the pinched and deeply stressful state of dependent poor families can have an impact on youth crime in fairly short order," he wrote in his *Working Papers* article. One comprehensive federal initiative for high-risk families that Currie endorses is called Child and Family Resource Programs, one element in Washington's still nascent efforts in the area of family-support systems. At fifteen experimental CFRP centers around the country, services as varied as crisis intervention, education against child abuse, family counseling, Head Start and tutoring programs, meals for children and pre- and post-natal health counseling are all combined.

Currie points out that the General Accounting Office, no soft touch for social programs, gave CFRPs high grades when it studied them in 1979. For a cost of about $3,000 per family, GAO concluded, the CFRPs not only improved the quality of life in poor families but also had the potential to head off future costs to society in such areas as health care, welfare assistance and youth and adult corrections. "The GAO argued," Currie writes, "that these early childhood intervention programs would reduce delinquency mainly through improving early parent-child relations and school performance, and both possibilities fit well with what a growing body of research has to say about family and developmental influences on youth and adult crime." Dr. Edward Zigler, a Yale psychologist and longtime advocate of family support systems, says that programs of this kind have a proven record for reducing the stress in low-income families. "Anything that cuts down on the amount of stress on these families helps them," he said, "and cuts down on violence."

Programs like family-support systems, Chapter 1 basic-skills instruction in the schools and the combined education-employment effort envisioned by the Carter administration have so far been limited in scope and results. But now that the country has the benefit of eighteen years of experience with federal programs of this kind, one cannot say flatly that these are things that government simply cannot do well. There have been some success stories. Controversy over such programs will continue, but it will likely focus on the extent to which they should be expanded and how they may be improved. Supporters of federal intervention will argue that these programs have demonstrated potential to improve the quality of life for many citizens—and to expand job opportunities in places where crime is now the equal opportunity employer of last resort.

looted grocery store

Chapter 4

"Where justice is denied"

Where justice is denied, where any one class is
made to feel that society is an organized conspiracy
to oppress and rob and degrade them, neither
persons nor property will be safe.

> —*Frederick Douglass, black author and
> abolitionist of the nineteenth century.*

If we had street crime in suburbia, I suspect that we
would solve it.

> —*The Reverend Buck Jones,
> East St. Louis, Illinois*

here are great potential mis-
understandings when the special role of race is considered in the
crime problem of the United States. Among them is the perception
that any attention focused on the disproportionately high arrest
rates of minority-group members inevitably reflects racial or ethnic
stereotyping, if not outright scapegoating of blacks or Hispanic
Americans.

The risk of such misunderstandings exists, but the effort to
explore this issue must be made nonetheless. The American problem
of racial injustice is simply too tightly interwoven with the American
problem of crime. While criminologist Norval Morris of the
University of Chicago can talk perceptively of the fact that because
of the regional differences in incidence of crime the United States
really has many crime rates, it would be the worst folly for the
country to act as though the higher rate of crime in the inner city
were not a national problem for all Americans to confront.

For some time after crime rates, especially in the big cities, began to soar during the 1960s, mainstream politicians in the United States did tend to ignore the problem. They did this for a number of reasons, one of which was that there was great suspicion at the time (it was later shown to be largely unfounded) that the FBI Uniform Crime Report was exaggerating crime rates. Another factor though in most politicians' tendency during the 1960s to pay little heed to this problem or to respond to it solely with appeals for more government social programs was the feeling that complaints of "crime in the streets" were really just a disguised expression of general hostility toward blacks on the part of white racists.

What changed the politicians' attitude, in part, was the increasingly vocal concern of blacks themselves about high crime rates in their own neighborhoods. In *Thinking About Crime*, James Q. Wilson points out how evident blacks' frustration with crime had become before politicians (with such exceptions as George Wallace) began taking the problem seriously. Wilson mentions opinion polling that a colleague and he did in Boston in 1966. By that time, he said, blacks—as well as whites—were mentioning crime or urban disorder of one kind or another as the biggest problem facing the city. Moreover, Wilson discovered, those whites who said that government should do more to help blacks were just as likely to complain about crime or other undesirable behavior in public as those whites who said the government had already done too much. Lamenting crime was not just a cover for antiblack sentiments. A *Fortune* magazine survey of 1,300 black males in 1968 came up with much the same conclusion: Blacks felt victimized by crime and wanted something done about it. By that time, Wilson says, politicians with more sensitive antennae (he mentions Robert Kennedy in particular) were beginning to realize that this was not a white versus black issue but a whites and blacks versus criminals issue.

Clearing the air on this point had one advantage in particular: It let everyone talk more openly about the real dimensions of the crime that is done to and by blacks. In 1981, blacks, who make up about 12 percent of the population, accounted for 34.1 percent of all crime arrests, 45.7 percent of all violent-crime arrests. Blacks are two and a half times as likely to be victims of violent crimes as whites. The ABC-News poll on crime found that nearly three-fourths of the black population of the United States have been victims of one kind of crime or another. Homicide is the leading cause of death among young black males. Babies born and raised in U.S. cities, Massachusetts Institute of Technology researchers calculated, are more likely to be murdered than GIs who served in World War II were to die in combat.

The broken
mobility escalator

One explanation of this phenomenon is that blacks are simply going through the same experience that other newcomers to the nation's big cities have gone through. At various times, Irish, German, Jewish and Italian immigrants all flooded to these shores and temporarily sent local crime rates soaring. According to this theory, the problem will disappear as the economy works its magical effects on blacks and moves them up the ladder of social mobility and into the middle class. (Indeed, millions of blacks *have* joined the middle class and, predictably enough, their crime rate is much lower than that of lower-class blacks.) Wilson describes this process in *Thinking About Crime*, with particular reference to his own nineteenth century immigrant Irish forebears: "By the end of the century the jails and poorhouses were filled with Irishmen (probably including some ancestor of mine), and demands were heard for an end to immigration. Within a few decades, however, the crime rates had fallen dramatically as acculturation worked its way. There is as yet no reason to suppose that this process will not also operate in the decades ahead."

Would that it were so. But eight years after Wilson wrote that in 1975, the official unemployment rate of black teenagers is close to 50 percent. Between 1971 and 1980, the percentage of blacks living below the poverty line did not change by so much as one-tenth of 1 percent: It has remained more than 32 percent for the decade. The great escalator of the American system is clearly stalled.

Why that is so is a question that has occupied some of the country's most astute minds for years. Two of the more insightful books on the subject are Charles E. Silberman's *Crisis in Black and White* and *Criminal Violence, Criminal Justice*. His description of the problem relates blacks' history of subjugation and lack of economic progress directly to the feelings of despair and futurelessness that are so much a part of ghetto life.

Silberman argues persuasively what he and other black and white observers have made so abundantly clear: The black experience in America has been radically different from that of any other immigrant group. No other Americans were taken from their homeland and forced to come to this country; no others lived for generations under the degrading circumstances of slavery; and no other minority has suffered for so long and at such intense levels the economic and social effects of a prejudice that is all the more irrationally virulent and persistent because it is based on a physical characteristic. Silberman quotes to good effect the prescience of Alexis de Tocqueville writing long before Emancipation: "Slavery recedes, but the prejudice to which it has given birth is immovable." And, "To induce whites to abandon the opinion they have conceived of the moral and intellectual inferiority of their former slaves, the Negroes must change, but as long as this opinion persists, they cannot change."

The prejudice of whites toward blacks in both the North and the South is what kept black Americans after the Civil War from following the path of upward mobility that had been taken by other newcomers to industrializing America. Silberman substantiates this with reference to the study of social mobility in Boston done by Stephan Thernstrom in *The Other Bostonians*. In 1860, Thernstrom's data showed that blacks occupied a higher occupational status in Boston than the new arrivals from Ireland. Yet by 1890, 32 percent of Irish second-generation workers held white-collar jobs and just 17 percent of second-generation blacks did. Perhaps the best proof that it was racial prejudice and not any objective difference in ability that held blacks back is the fact that while blacks were hired in substantial numbers for unskilled positions, employers systematically hired whites for the semiskilled jobs in the same industries—even though the semiskilled work did not require a higher level of education, discipline or skill. Throughout the last decades of the nineteenth century and the first decades of this century, blacks were regularly displaced from occupations, such as locomotive fireman or carpenter, in which they had at one time been prominently represented. Additional proof that blacks had been kept out of certain occupations by prejudice alone was provided by World War II. In a time of manpower shortages, blacks successfully filled industrial jobs that had previously been denied them.

The breakdown of
social controls

Silberman's work is particularly illuminating in describing the defenses that blacks developed as a response to this treatment and to the violence, disenfranchisement and segregation that was their lot at the hands of whites in the South. The effect of those defenses and the broader social controls that grew out of them was to keep black resentment from turning violent. "Black Americans," Silberman writes in *Criminal Violence, Criminal Justice*, "had to invent ways of channeling their anger and controlling their hate; they had to create non-suicidal forms of courage. Had they not done so, the United States would have gone up in smoke long ago. What has happened in the last fifteen years, in good measure, is that the cultural devices that kept black violence under control have broken down, and that new cultural controls have not yet emerged."

To the extent that some of these controls required blacks in effect to swallow their racial pride, the 1960s changes that Silberman describes had some indisputably positive features. Elijah Anderson of the University of Pennsylvania offers a good description of the transformation in his essay, "Some Observations of Black Youth Unemployment," which appeared in Bernard E. Anderson and Isabel V. Sawhill's *Youth Employment and Public Policy*: "All of these themes came together and generated among young blacks a new sense of self-worth. Young blacks often accepted this theme as a kind of license 'to be yourself' and to loosen the bonds of dominant social institutions, eschewing their symbolic forms such as conventional dress and hairstyles. It was in these circumstances that formal and informal agencies of socialization and social control came into question. Many of the young began to dispute the authority of the police, educators, their elders and others."

Anderson's essay is a well-rounded summary of both the difficulties that urban black males have fitting in to the legitimate economy and the temptations and opportunities that are offered by "hustling" and crime. The unwillingness of many young blacks to conform to conventional notions of proper dress or demeanor on the job has combined with employers' distrust of blacks to create prickly personnel relations that are one factor, Anderson indicates, in the pattern of "serial employment" of young black employees. As Anderson points out, in white-white situations, a request to a worker that he conform to a dress code is not a racial issue. "But," he writes, "given the background of the 1960s and the history of racial prejudice in America, the same request made by a white boss to a young black person often leads to charges of prejudice and racial slight."

Anderson describes the frustrations of young blacks who find themselves bouncing from one job to another, often positions that many of the youths consider beneath their own real worth. Young whites, Anderson points out, can accept with reasonably good grace menial work with the realization that it is only a temporary way station en route to one of the higher-status jobs that confer the material and psychological reward that young people of both races aspire to. For blacks, reconciling themselves to menial jobs that they know will lead nowhere does not come easily. "While they desire 'good' jobs," Anderson writes of young blacks, "many sorely lack basic skills, including the ability to read and write and to perform even rudimentary computations. While possessing the high-school diploma of the segregated urban school system, many have never acquired a basic level of education. Nonetheless, many feel they are qualified for jobs better than those they are able to obtain."

This attitude leads to an ambivalence in youths when employers lay them off or fire them: Some, according to Anderson, "view it as a kind of blessing." Unemployment confirms their feelings about white society and its institutions and, in Anderson's phrase, "predisposes many to move in the direction many of their unemployed peers like to see them go—toward the underground economy."

Taking pride in "getting by"

Anderson describes the way many black youths try to make a virtue out of the adversity of unemployment by pretending to themselves, in a sour grapes reaction, that "getting by" without work is laudable—even if, or especially if, this necessitates criminal activities. In some cases, this defense reaction can grow so strong that a young black can begin to define himself as someone of worth precisely because he is a person "who ain't got to work."

Deprived of the status that a "good" job provides, black youths often seek it, Anderson says, through possession of the large amounts of money that hustling or street crime can provide. Money takes on a value of its own. In 1979, New York police arrested a young black robber, Clifford Brightman, who, in the course of confessing to his latest crime on a police videotape, also boasted about the fact that he had $9,000 in his pocket before he began the last heist: "Before I went to stick up the store, I had $9,000 in my pocket... In brand new crispy $100 bills I had in my pocket, up to today." Later in the tape, he said, "I had big knots in my pocket. When I went to the movies and see that picture, 'The Man,' I said to be black and rich means something."

Rufus Saunders, a thirty-two-year-old black with an extensive police record, recalled in an interview with ABC News the pressure he felt as a young man to win the esteem of his friends: "Everybody wants to be recognized. Okay? On what level depends on the individual. But, in my era, being recognized meant dressing, having your own money and stealing and stuff of that nature." It was not enough for him, Saunders said, "to be wanted, loved and needed at my home. But I needed to be wanted, loved and needed in the streets, too. You know what I mean? I didn't want to go to school and have nobody take my lunch money. Okay? So, in order to keep people from taking my lunch money, I look somebody else's lunch money. And if I take somebody else's lunch money, now I'm tough. Okay?"

Anderson's detailed view of the attitudes and prospects of young blacks is not entirely bleak. He points out, for instance, that the hope of a rewarding job can spring eternal even in the breast of marginal street criminals. Many, he says, will go looking for a job when they hear one is available. This helps to confirm the conclusion of Robert L. Green of the University of Michigan that, based on a survey done by Ohio State University for the U.S. Labor Department, there is no evidence of unwillingness to work on the part of minority-group youth.

In effect, Anderson proposes that U.S. society offer something approaching a new deal to the young black underclass. Society needs to provide job skills and training and more meaningful jobs, not make-work ones, with realistic hope of advancement. In the previous chapter, sociologist Elliott Currie was quoted making the same point: dead end, low-wage jobs will not suffice. Beyond that, Anderson says, employers must show greater tolerance and understanding for the "status problems" of young black workers. It is a tall order, but it is no more formidable than the cost to society if it continues to do nothing about its alienated and resentful minority.

Their own neighborhood

As much as blacks long for the racial justice that may one day assure their youth of futures more promising than what they now have to look forward to, they also often have to live in the very neighborhoods that are most victimized by black criminals. While there are, of course, more adventurous criminals who will leave their own, usually low-income area to prey on a more affluent part of the city, the great majority of criminals do their robbing and burglarizing quite close to where they live. Police in New York City have based a very successful antirobbery program, discussed more fully in the next chapter, on this fact.

Programs like New York's provide a dividend above and beyond the numbers of robbers that are captured or crimes deterred. Such programs also help to redress minority groups' long-standing grievance that police officers—and society as a whole—have paid too little attention to the crime problems that beset many minority communities, from Washington, D.C., to East Los Angeles. It is a common complaint. Back in the 1960s, when James Q. Wilson studied police practices in several different cities for his book, *Varieties of Police Behavior*, he found this opinion particularly pronounced in Newburgh, New York. "In Newburgh," he wrote, "every Negro interviewed—lawyers, ministers, night-club owners, prostitutes—agreed that the overriding characteristic of the Newburgh police was their tendency to under-enforce the law in Negro areas." Wilson linked this criticism of the Newburgh police to what he called its "watchman" style, a preference for ignoring minor matters but getting tough when "something important is at stake." Obviously, what may seem like minor misdemeanors to a police officer may look to a resident of the area where the misdemeanors occur like an unacceptable breach of public order.

John Dean, a black who serves on the Crime Compensation Board in Washington, D.C., discussed the gap between whites' and blacks' experience of crime in an ABC News interview: "It's very difficult to live outside of a black community and perceive of the thinking and feeling that goes on inside... It is that all-pervasive fear because you never know, as I say, when you step out whether you're going to come back, and mostly when you're even in your house you don't have that sense of security that the majority population takes for granted."

Victimized by crime in this way, blacks in many cities have turned their neighborhood or community organizations into vehicles for anticrime activities, from street patrols to neighborhood watches to lobbying their police departments for more protection. In other cities, minority-group members are using existing organizations or starting new ones as an alternative to gang life or street crime for their unemployed youth. To the extent that such organizations work, it is probably because they are staffed and led by individuals who have come up through the same circumstances as the young men and can tell them, as the leader of a center in Phoenix, Arizona, *barrio* put it, "that there's other things out there in life."

In the crime poll, more than half the blacks sampled thought that the best protection against crime was some form of a neighborhood crime-watch program. As will be discussed in Chapter 6, such efforts are also becoming increasingly popular in white, middle-class communities.

But there is a special poignancy to programs like the one run by the North Michigan Park Civic Association in heavily black northeast Washington, D.C. At one meeting, a local civic official remarked, "The better crime-watch program you have in your community, the fewer youths will go to jail." When blacks or other minority-group members organize to prevent crime, they are trying to protect not just their property and their persons but the future of their young as well. The rest of society owes those minority families support, from well-run jobs programs to effective police protection. The minority-group crime problem is a national crime problem.

police
confrontation
at
demonstra

Chapter 5

The police: back to basics

You can't be in every place all the time. It's
virtually impossible. Even if you had a
policeman on every corner, I would venture to
say that you couldn't stop crime.
> —*Officer Paul Dominick of the*
> *Chicago Police Department*

here are more than 400,000 police
officers in the United States. Working for 18,000 different departments or agencies, they patrol streets, investigate crimes and—
when they are lucky—make arrests. But for all their efforts, they
haven't stopped crime in this country, and, as Officer Paul
Dominick of the Chicago Police Department says, even satura-
tion patrolling would not end crime problems.

There is probably no police chief anywhere in the United States
who wouldn't like to have a bigger force than he has now. But if a
chief's mayor or city council told him he could hire and keep a
new contingent of officers only on the condition that the city's
crime rate show a proportionate drop, any honest chief would
have to say it's a deal he couldn't sign.

The high-crime years that began in the 1960s and seem to have
peaked in 1980 were tough on many of the long-held beliefs that

underlay crime-fighting in the United States. The sharp increases in crime during that period were one factor that led many Americans to subject police departments to the same kind of scrutiny that was being applied to Great Society programs or the military-industrial complex. Private research groups, such as the Police Foundation established by the Ford Foundation in 1970, INSLAW (originally called the Institute of Law and Social Research) founded in 1972 and the Police Executive Research Forum established in 1976, began to explore the question of how police might become more effective in the diverse roles that are expected of them.

Over the years, those roles have changed, but the changes have often been less pronounced than the perceptions of police work that the public and police officers themselves have had. Police departments were first set up in the 1830s and 1840s in large eastern cities like Boston and New York as organizations of municipal watchmen hired to keep some semblance of order during an era of frequent riots, brawling and public drunkenness. In this century, and especially since World War II, policemen have defined themselves more and more as society's professional crime-fighters. Television and the movies, needless to say, have helped to foster this self-image, even though it conflicts with the reality that police devote on average about 20 percent of their time to crime-related functions and spend the majority of their time on service calls or on order-maintenance activities—like a nineteenth-century watchman-policeman.

Crime-fighters or keepers of order?

The public contributes to this gap between police officers' definition of themselves as crime-fighters and the actual ways in which they spend their time. An ABC-News poll showed that 69 percent considers "preventing and solving crimes" as the main job of the police, yet 72 percent would call the police to handle "a noisy late-night argument between a husband and wife."

A policeman's role as keeper of order and provider of emergency services can often effectively complement his role as crime-fighter. Only a very small percentage of all arrests develop out of police responses to in-progress crimes. According to a four-city Police Executive Research Forum study on police response to crime reports, in just 2.9 percent of such cases is the criminal nabbed. Research by Albert Reiss of Yale has shown that honest-to-goodness criminal incidents come to the attention of police less than 1 percent of the time they are on patrol. In the vast majority of arrests, victims or witnesses are able to give a partial or full identification of the suspect. In other cases, crimes are solved or "cleared" when informants, sometimes criminals themselves, provide tips or when suspects are arrested and make a clean breast of a whole roster of past transgressions. This information-collecting function of a police officer is enhanced when, because of other contacts he has made in his patrol area, he is known to and trusted by potential sources of crime-related information. To quote Officer Dominick of the Chicago Police Department again, "It's a 99 percent people-oriented type job." Much of the recent experimentation in police operations has been with an eye toward making the different roles of the police officer dovetail more effectively than they have in the past.

One fact that quickly became apparent as researchers looked into police work is that there is little safety in numbers. While the average city with a population of more than 250,000 has 3.4 policemen per 1,000 residents, the ratio for individual cities ranges from 1.7 to 7 policemen per 1,000 citizens. Such wide disparities should account for substantial differences in crime rates, but they don't. As Charles Silberman notes in *Criminal Violence, Criminal Justice*: "There is no observable correlation between the number of police a community has and either the number of crimes that are committed or the proportion of those crimes that are solved."

Just as sheer numbers of police don't necessarily reduce the crime rate, the technical gadgetry that police have at their disposal doesn't seem to make much of a dent in the problem, either. The best illustration of this is the hundreds of millions of dollars frittered away in the 1970s by the federal Law Enforcement Assistance Administration on riot guns, fancy radios and even, in some cases, helicopters. The LEAA was by no means a total loss. In many jurisdictions, it provided funds for faster and more effective prosecution of criminal cases in court, an approach that can be more useful in fighting crime than simply beefing up police departments. Moreover, it was with an LEAA contract that the Census Bureau began conducting crime-victimization surveys aimed at checking the accuracy of the crime figures collected from local departments by the Federal Bureau of Investigation and published by the FBI in its annual *Uniform Crime Reports*. LEAA-sponsored research into specific areas of crime, such as juvenile delinquency, did add to the public's overall knowledge. Still, the demise of the agency was little mourned when the Reagan administration stopped funding for it in 1982.

When speed isn't of the essence

Another challenge to conventional wisdom in crime-fighting came with the discovery in recent years that a police department's response time is of precious little consequence if, as is often the case, the victims of crimes are delaying their calls to the police. What studies have found is that there is a significant lag between the moment of the crime and the time when the victim has sufficiently recovered from the shock of the robbery or assault to call the police. Often, the victim's first instinct is to call a close relative or friend. The Police Executive Research Forum's 1981 response-time survey turned up average reporting delays by citizens of 4 to 5.5 minutes, even for crimes in which the complainants had been involved, as opposed to burglaries, for instance, that had been discovered after the fact. A police rule of thumb is that an on-scene arrest is possible only if police themselves can reach the scene within two or three minutes of the crime.

This doesn't suggest that police should be lackadaisical about responding to reports of crimes. Prompt questioning of the victim is useful if only to get his description of the incident and the criminal while the facts are still fresh in his mind. But if a department's insistence on fast response times means that the officer dispatched to the scene is often one called in from a different patrol area (because the local patrolman is already on a call), that investigating officer is less likely to be familiar with the victim's neighborhood or the criminals operating in it. As a result, his interview with the victim will probably be less productive than it would have been if it had been conducted by the beat patrolman. The simplest way for a police dispatcher to determine if speed is in fact of the essence in police response to a crime is to ask the victim how much time has elapsed since the crime has occurred. An increasing number of departments are reported to be screening calls in this way.

Fast response time is very much to be desired in crimes such as bank robberies, where the report of the victim is almost instantaneous and there is, in many cases, a realistic chance of catching the robber red-handed. But it is probably a mistake for police departments to set standards and organization procedures with an eye toward a type of crime that is comparatively rare—especially if those procedures get in the way of the most effective handling of crimes that are of greater concern to the citizen.

Doubts about preventive patrol

The survey on victim delay in reporting crime cast doubt on one shibboleth of police operations— the all-importance in every crime call of the fastest possible response. But that wasn't the first time that field research had undercut faith in established police procedure. Earlier, in 1972 and 1973, a study in Kansas City challenged police administrators' longstanding belief in the usefulness of patrol in cruisers, the bread-and-butter crime-prevention activity of most police departments. The experiment was initiated in 1972, when the chief of the Kansas City department was Clarence M. Kelley. Kelley left before the test period was completed to become director of the Federal Bureau of Investigation and was succeeded by Joseph D. McNamara.

The designers of the Kansas City study, which was funded by the Police Foundation, focused on a part of the city with fifteen beats. Those fifteen were randomly divided into three groups. In five "reactive" beats, routine patrol was ended altogether and police entered the areas only to answer service calls. In five "control" beats, regular patrol coverage of one car per beat was maintained. In the other five "proactive" beats, patrol was increased to two or three times its normal level with extra cruisers and the presence of cars from the underserved "reactive" beats.

The results of the year-long trial were eye-opening. Tallies of both reported crime and victimization surveys showed that the differences in patrolling had no significant effect on the incidence of precisely those crimes, such as robberies, burglaries and auto thefts, that preventive patrolling is supposed to deter. Furthermore, citizens' fear of crime throughout the test area was unaffected by the different levels of patrolling. Overall, citizen satisfaction with police service was unrelated to the experimental conditions.

When news of these results first came to the attention of the media, their meaning and import were often twisted or inflated. The Kansas City experiment did *not* necessarily present an argument for smaller police forces. What the experiment did indicate was that police administrators could safely reduce preventive patrols and deploy their officers in other, more innovative ways. Even this reading of the Kansas City experiment, however, represented a reversal in what had been police dogma. The late O.W. Wilson, a former chief of the Chicago Police Department and an academic specialist in police matters, was a leading advocate of the traditional view of patrol: By creating an impression of police omnipresence, he said, it could deter would-be offenders and was, in general, an "indispensable service that plays a leading role in the accomplishment of the police purpose."

But if cruiser patrol is not a very effective use of police time, what is? Thoughtful police officials in a wide range of communities have experimented with different answers to this question. One approach has been to assign more officers to special crime details in decoy or surveillance situations. For cities that have clearly identifiable "hot spots" of crime, this use of manpower may prove quite effective.

In the spring of 1981, when statistics showed robberies in New York City increasing at a rate that was way out of proportion to the overall increase in crime, that city's police department decided to deploy 1,400 officers in areas with particularly high robbery rates. By the spring of 1983, that concentration was credited as one factor in a decline of 10.7 percent in robberies during 1982. Crime overall in New York City declined 5.1 percent in that year.

New York police officials think the focus on robberies may have helped reduce the incidence of other crimes, too. "Most robbers are criminal opportunists," said Inspector James Trainor, commander of the central robbery division. "They will rip off an old lady on the street, go through a window of a house to commit a burglary or steal a car. When you put somebody away for robbery, you may be putting away somebody who already has or will eventually commit other kinds of crime."

In general, Trainor finds specialized anticrime details "tremendously effective." His estimate is that while the plainclothes officers on anticrime assignments make up less than 10 percent of the entire department, they account for about 40 percent of all felony arrests. There are, he said, officers who are particularly adept at this kind of work, the "super cops" who are responsible for greatly disproportionate numbers of a department's arrests. "There's definitely such a thing as 'street eyes,'" Trainor said. "It's a quality that most police officers have, but some have them to the nth degree."

New York's Robbery
Identification Program

While robbery rates dropped 10.7 percent citywide in New York in 1982, the decline was even steeper (16.2 percent) in six precincts where robbery had been a particularly severe problem. For department officials like Trainor, these results were no surprise. Those six precincts had been try-out spots for one of the more promising big-city efforts to make a major dent in the street-crime problem.

It's called the Robbery Identification Program. Based on the knowledge that "the same perps (perpetrators) frequent the same areas," as Trainor puts it, New York has begun localizing the process of identifying and catching robbery suspects. Instead of taking robbery complainants or witnesses to the borough's computerized mug-shot facility four or five precincts away (which is the usual routine), the first officer who responds to a robbery call in a precinct with an RIP system brings the citizen immediately to the precinct station. There the victim or witness is presented with a manageable number of mug shots of known robbers from the sector within the precinct where the crime took place. To narrow the selection down even further, detectives will quiz the citizen about the race, height, age and identifying features or techniques of the robber. It can mean that the citizen is looking at as few as thirty or forty mug shots, Trainor said. Deputy Inspector John J. Hill, commander of the 90th Precinct in Brooklyn, where the program got its initial try-out in December of 1981, told a *New York Times* reporter: "So why should the victim have to go look at thousands of mug shots of robbers who come from all over the borough? Why not start with the bad guys in your own neighborhood?" This process alone, Trainor said, can produce a "hit rate" of positive identifications of 20 percent, far higher than usual.

"It's amazing," Hill told the *Times*, "but we found that robbers rarely go more than one or two sectors (the 90th Precinct has been divided into seven sectors) away from where they live." Precinct officers had noted, he said, that the middle-class sectors within the 90th experienced relatively few robberies "because the robbers live in the poorer neighborhoods and rob there. They don't cross lines." A further reason that RIP precincts have better luck in identification is that there is no delay between the time of the crime and the victim's viewing of the mug shots, as there often is in precincts without the program.

More effective use of mug shots is just part of RIP. When an identification is made and the suspect cannot immediately be found, the suspect's mug shots are displayed on a bulletin board that is seen by the precinct's uniformed officers. To demonstrate how much importance the department places on capturing robbery suspects, precinct commanders are authorized to issue an officer an "exceptional police duty" award when he or she has collared two of them. Another aspect of the program is the establishment, within each precinct's detective unit, of a special group of twelve to fourteen who concentrate solely on robberies. This, Trainor said, helps the remaining detectives in the precinct because it allows them to concentrate on homicides and rapes without having to concern themselves with robberies. The robbery detectives naturally develop considerable expertise about the methods and preferred locales of robbers in the precinct.

Various elements of RIP, Trainor was quick to point out, have been used on a formal or informal basis elsewhere in New York and, undoubtedly, in other cities, as well. "This is not new, new stuff, it's not revolutionary," said Trainor. "It's a common-sense approach. We put it all together to make an RIP system."

The statistics on what they put together are eye-opening. After beginning the program in Brooklyn's 90th Precinct, the department was so impressed by its initial success that it quickly expanded the program to five more precincts in every borough except Staten Island in the spring of 1982 and hopes to have a dozen high-robbery-rate precincts organized this way before long. The payoff has not been just a steep decline in the robbery rate. While the city overall was reporting a 4.8 percent decline in robbery arrests in 1982, the RIP precincts—over the months that the program was in effect—showed an increase of 6.2 percent. In the city, the ratio of arrests to robbery complaints was 1 to 4.5 in 1982; in the RIP precincts, it was 1 to 3.9. Another dividend from the program has been fewer homicides. In 1982, the city homicide rate fell 8.6 percent; the RIP precincts' rate fell 11.2 percent—a reflection, Trainor said, of the fact that 20 percent of the city's homicides are robbery-related.

An RIP is not necessarily the answer for all police departments. But, for big cities that may be suffering from too much centralization of their police operations, something like RIP is an excellent way to cut a robbery problem down to size by confronting it on its own, local terms. "I think," said Trainor, "that we have the best system, with the most common sense, in the whole country."

The return to the walking beat

In other cities, disenchantment with cruiser patrol has caused police officials to consider more widespread use of that most basic of all police methods, the foot patrol. While foot patrol is probably ill-suited for newer cities of low residential and commercial density, in the older congested cities of the East and Midwest foot patrol has appealed to many police administrators as a crime-prevention measure and an effective way to maintain order in crowded urban situations. Furthermore, foot patrol is frequently suggested by urban citizens as a solution to the crime problems they see around them. In his preface to a report on a foot-patrol experiment in Newark, New Jersey, Police Foundation President Patrick Murphy points out that "citizens associate the officer on the foot beat with a time when crime rates were low and they felt secure in their neighborhoods."

A chance to determine whether this public enthusiasm for foot patrol was based on sound reason or just nostalgia came in the late 1970s after the state of New Jersey in 1973 had created a Safe and

Clean Neighborhoods Program. A portion of the funding went toward the establishment of new police foot patrols in twenty-eight cities, including Newark, where Murphy's Police Foundation did a study on the patrols' effectiveness.

On one level, the experiment results were discouraging: The patrols did not appear to affect crime levels, up or down, as measured both by reported crime and crime-victimization surveys. On another level, the patrols did exactly what they were supposed to: Citizen *perception* of crime did go down. According to George L. Kelling, who wrote the conclusions of the survey report: "Consistently, residents in beats where foot patrol was added see the severity of crime problems diminishing in their neighborhoods.... Street disorders, serious crime, drug usage, vandalism, victimization of the elderly and auto theft all are perceived to be less of a problem." In a result related to this one, residents of foot-beat areas also reported a decrease in their fear of crime. The foot patrols appear to yield another benefit as well in the attitudes of the officers who walk the beats. According to Kelling: "Foot patrol officers surveyed in New Jersey generally seem to have higher levels of job satisfaction, a more benign view of citizens and a more community-oriented view of policing than their colleagues on motor patrol."

Kelling's conclusions in the Newark report include a description of how one foot patrolman handled a beat that included one of the busiest intersections of the city, as well as the city's main bus transfer point. As Kelling points out: "If that downtown was to survive, people had to be comfortable using that intersection." The foot officer, to whom Kelling in his account gave the name "Kelly," worked effectively to make people comfortable in that area—despite the presence of a large number of street people. "Kelly" worked out rules for street behavior: Drunks or addicts could sit on store stoops but could not lie down; bottles could be carried in brown paper bags and people could drink on the street, but not at the main intersection; persons using the bus transfer points could not be hassled or panhandled.

None of this would necessarily prevent a major crime from taking place. But this foot patrolman's "order maintenance" is exactly what so many older and more vulnerable citizens of large cities miss in their neighborhoods and in the commercial areas where they must do business or run errands. As Kelling points out:

"... public disorder and strangers on streets generate as much fear as crime itself, and maybe more, and attempts to manage public order are, perhaps, as essential to reducing fear as to reducing crime."

In another city that has made extensive use of foot patrols, Flint, Michigan, tentative indications are that the patrols may have achieved what they did not in Newark—an actual reduction in crime. According to local figures, major crime in that city of high auto-industry unemployment increased since 1978, when the foot-patrol experiment began. But in the areas with policemen walking a beat, crime fell an average of 27 percent.

As in other cities that have tried foot patrols, the police in Flint were skeptical when the experiment began in 1978. Two years later, that attitude changed overnight. A policeman had shot and killed a black teenager, and tensions in the city were high. Shortly after that shooting, police called to a double murder at a bar found themselves surrounded by a hostile, rock-throwing mob. At that point, however, foot patrolmen from the neighborhood came in, talked with the angry citizens and took the edge off the situation.

The citizens of Flint had a chance to show their support for foot patrols in 1982. Money for the patrols had begun to run out, and the city had to decide whether to drop the program or raise taxes to maintain it. Despite a depression-level unemployment rate in the city, the voters chose by an overwhelming margin to raise their property taxes. Not only did they keep the foot patrols, they doubled them.

If foot patrols can be an effective way to hold down crime, Sergeant Steve Buzsek of the Flint Police Department probably touched on the reason why when he said: "I think people are more apt to get involved with someone they know on the police department than they are with someone they don't know. Like I say, I've worked this area of town for many, many years and I've made quite a few good arrests based on information from other people out here. And without that information, I wouldn't have had those good arrests."

Kelling, in his conclusions to the Newark study, makes the same point: The foot patrol's potential for developing good community relations makes it an effective way to gather information to help officers contend with neighborhood crime. The policeman's functions of providing public service, maintaining order and fighting crime need not be mutually exclusive.

Team-policing

Special crime details and foot patrols are just two of the ways that police administrators have tried to use their officers more productively. A third innovation has been called, for want of a better term, "team-policing." In this approach, departments get away from the specialized functions that much police work has been divided into with special juvenile, narcotics or community-relations units and instead leave virtually all of the responsibilities to a team of officers who are assigned to one specific area. The theory behind team-policing is that officers will be more effective if they are performing several complementary functions—taking crime reports, doing investigations, lecturing neighborhood groups on anticrime measures.

While team-policing has been tried in one form or another in several cities, it received its most formal test in Cincinnati during the early 1970s. The experiment was known as Comsec, for Community Sector Policing Project, and was limited to the city's District 1, its downtown and inner-city area. The district was divided into six sectors, each with its own team and team leader, a lieutenant. With the exception of homicide investigation and special crowd control duties (Cincinnati's Riverside Stadium is in the district), the teams were responsible for all police work in their sectors. To minimize the problem of team officers being summoned over to other sectors on service calls, the department introduced new dispatching techniques, including the "stacking" of calls that were not emergencies.

In several respects the new system worked well. Team leaders had greater freedom to set manpower schedules according to the actual needs of a sector and more flexibility was shown in making decisions about patrolling. Perhaps because of better patrolling, the burglary rate in the district went down.

By other measures, however, it would be difficult to call Comsec a success. Rates of crimes other than burglary did not fall in District 1, there was little or no improvement in the community's attitude toward the police and, by the end of the thirty-month trial period, friction within the department over the team leaders' autonomy had led to moves that reduced their authority and undercut much of the "team" style. One explanation for the lack of any decided improvement in community relations is that, notwithstanding a good deal of departmental rhetoric on this score, officers still felt pressures to issue a certain number of tickets or make a certain number of arrests. Not only did these activities take up time that might more usefully have been spent developing productive ties with the community, but the tickets and arrests also made it difficult for sector residents to see much difference between Comsec's team policemen and the patrolmen they had known before. The lesson of Comsec seemed to be that team-policing might work, but it requires thoroughgoing changes in departmental procedures and attitudes.

Other cities have met the challenge of improving the links between police and the community in different ways. In the mid-1970s, the city of Santa Ana, California, responded to accelerating rates of crime by setting up a program called Community-Oriented Policing. COP, as it is called, recruited civilians to serve as auxiliaries for Santa Ana's regular police officers. The civilians were given uniforms and a badge, but no guns, and were taught how to handle many of the duties that fill up a police officer's day but have little to do with fighting crime. COP workers investigate traffic accidents, write up accident reports, interview burglary victims. While earning one-third less than the regular policemen, they free the officers for higher-priority work. Not the least of the advantages of this new infusion of assistants from the city's neighborhoods is that they improve communication between the department and the community. As one officer told a group of new COP workers: "We want you guys to be the eyes and ears of the Santa Ana Police Department. We want you guys helping us help you."

Within two years of COP's establishment, Santa Ana's rate of crime increase went from the highest in the state to the lowest. It may have just been coincidental that this occurred at the same time as COP drew more Santa Ana citizens into the police department, but probably not. The evidence is strong that, in the short run or the long run, police departments that manage in one way or another to work themselves into the fabric of their communities are going to do a better job at *all* the duties citizens expect of their men and women in blue.

The "broken window"
phenomenon

In the 1960s, Harvard Professor James Q. Wilson took a look at eight of this country's thousands of police departments and noticed something that should have been obvious but had never been so clearly analyzed: Police departments have different styles, styles that are dependent on their cities' histories, ethnic make-ups, political environments and, in some cases, the personalities of the police or political leaders. While Wilson, in *Varieties of Police Behavior*, divided the departments he studied into three broad groups, the larger point is that no two departments are quite the same. To paraphrase what House Speaker Thomas P. O'Neill Jr. said about politics, "All police work is local."

By the same token, no two departments will likely respond to the public's frustration with high crime rates in the same way. What works in one city could quite possibly be a bust in another. In a televised panel discussion as part of the ABC-News "Crime in America" series, Newark Police Director Hubert Williams and Joseph D. McNamara, chief of the San Jose, California, police department, disagreed on the usefulness of foot patrols. Williams defended them as a way to make citizens feel more secure in their neighborhoods; McNamara advocated what he sees as more "efficient programs": street-crime units, sting operations, decoys, home-alert programs, truancy-abatement programs.

What was interesting in their dialogue, however, is that neither would say much in favor of what has been the backbone of American police work—the motor patrol. The lesson of the 1972–73 Kansas City experiment has sunk in. Preventive patrol is not an effective way to deter crime. The other drawback to motor patrol is that in the way it is all too often handled it offers relatively few opportunities for the kinds of contacts with citizens that police depend on to serve both their crime-fighting and their order-maintenance functions. As Patrick Murphy says in his preface to the Police Foundation's report on the Newark experiment: "If citizens know and trust their police, particularly individual, familiar officers, they are more likely to provide information to those officers than they are to strangers in uniform who whiz by occasionally in patrol cars."

The discrediting of preventive patrol, that most explicitly crime-fighting activity of the police, has led many police officials and researchers to wonder if crime-fighting might be one of those situations in which the shortest distance between two points might *not* be a straight line. Crime can also be fought, especially in urban areas, by making sure that certain ground rules of city street life governing activities like panhandling are upheld. When those rules of civility and order are not maintained, would-be criminals are inevitably tempted to suspect, usually correctly, that other, more important rules can also be broken with impunity. In their article in the March 1982 issue of *Atlantic Monthly*, Kelling and Wilson refer to the "broken window" phenomenon: When one window of a building is broken and then not repaired, all the rest of the windows will soon be broken. By much the same process, obnoxious or bothersome public behavior, if nothing is done about it, can result in a collapse of those social controls that provide a community with its most basic defense against the criminal.

The police officer in a cruiser is a poor regulator of street behavior. His "steel cocoon" automatically isolates him from the life of the street. A foot patrolman or a community team policeman is in a much better position to determine what kind of standards should be set and then to enforce them.

No, a police officer cannot be on every corner. But it will be a sign of progress in many U.S. cities when now-fearful citizens feel that *they* can be on any corner without a high risk of being robbed, abused or accosted. And that will come about sooner if police bring old-time common sense to bear on such crimes as robbery with systems like New York's Robbery Identification Program. Police departments would also do well not to forget their watchman past. A campaign against disorder and unruliness can be a first line of defense against crime.

Chapter 6

NYC guardian angels

Vigilance, not vigilantism

I have been called the nosy neighbor now, which I
never was before, and I really don't care. I think
that's something we have to learn to live with.
Become a nosy neighbor. Care about your neighbor.
　　　　　—*Josephine Pasquale, organizer of a*
　　　　neighborhood crime-watch station in Detroit.

f you ask a police officer to draw
up a composite of a city area that has an unusually low crime rate,
some of the characteristics of that ideal neighborhood that he will
mention are that a high proportion of the families or individuals
have resided there for some time, that they watch out for each
other in many different ways and that, in general, the neighborhood is close-knit. This is, regrettably, a description of a way of
living that is all too rare these days. Americans are mobile people
who pull up stakes and sink new roots with remarkable frequency.
Our families are smaller than they were twenty-five years ago, and
the links that children create within a neighborhood are consequently not so extensive.

There have been other changes, too, in neighborhood life from
the low-crime years of the 1940s and 1950s. Television and air-
conditioning have made us indoor people, even in the summer

months when, not too many years ago, people used to spend so much of their time on front stoops or front porches. The racket of air-conditioners, televisions and stereos keeps us from hearing a lock being jimmied or a window forced; the declining popularity of the front porch in house design wiped out one of the most effective anticrime systems any neighborhood can have—watchful, knowledgeable people keeping an eye on the street's activities.

It is no easy matter to take a neighborhood that bears little resemblance to the ideal sketched above and re-create the conditions that make for a largely crime-free atmosphere. But for more than a decade now, Americans have been making that attempt on an organized basis. Whether it's in the form of actual citizen patrols or just neighborhood watches, the citizen movement to prevent crime is one of the most encouraging developments on the American scene. Such patrols and watches have been set up in more than 20,000 communities with an estimated five million volunteers.

Making Detroit safer

Detroit is one of the success stories of this program. In the early 1970s, Detroit was dubbed the murder capital of the United States, with an average of two people being killed every day. The city's police took a long, hard look at what they were doing and decided that it simply wasn't working. For want of any more promising approach, they began devoting some of their manpower to setting up neighborhood watches.

The first was in the Creary St. Mary's area of northwest Detroit. Four police officers went into the area, organized it and began training its residents in crime prevention. The lessons taught were the basic ones that have since then been given to millions of Americans: how to recognize a crime or a potential crime, how to describe the person involved, how to make homes more secure with better locks and better lighting and —most importantly— how to look out for others. When 50 percent of the homes on a given block had joined the program, a sign was posted proclaiming its participation.

The effort was not in vain. Before long, the test area was reporting a crime reduction of 60 or 61 percent, especially in the burglaries that had been a major problem in the area.

Since that first test, the program has become a mainstay of the Detroit Police Department. Although a budget squeeze in the last four years has caused the layoffs of 1,300 Detroit officers, the department nonetheless still assigns 165 men and women to its crime-prevention section. Of the 12,000 blocks in the city of Detroit, 4,200 have neighborhood watches that enroll 150,000 residents. In addition, the city also has a Citizen Radio Mobile Patrol, with 35 patrols and 2,000 volunteers.

The do-it-yourself spirit has spread into other activities, as well. Citizen volunteers will, on request, install secure locks in homes and mark valuables with identification numbers—with the city paying for the hardware. Other volunteers have agreed to escort the elderly back and forth to banks when their Social Security checks arrive.

The institution of one of the country's most ambitious citizen-watch programs is not the only change in the city's crime-fighting efforts in recent years. Detroit has also set up fifty police ministations to broaden the police department's presence throughout the city. "Today," says Inspector James Humphrey, commanding officer of the Detroit Crime Prevention Section, "with the fifty police ministations and with crime prevention being a priority, there is a strong positive relationship between the police and the community." Whatever the cause, Detroit's crime rate in the past ten years has fallen a remarkable 50 percent.

Police and citizen cooperation

Can citizen watches work anywhere? The answer is probaby yes, but don't expect immediate declines in reported crime. In many communities, the establishment of a neighborhood watch is promptly followed by an increase in reported crime. Many crimes that citizens had not previously reported out of sheer frustration with the criminal justice system *will* be reported when a citizen watch is on the scene. There are also certain conditions that help to assure the success of watch programs. Humphrey points to the importance of having a city's top police and civilian officials backing the program. He also warns that it is not easy, in some instances, to sell police officers themselves on the merits of the program. Going into a neighborhood and motivating residents to be more watchful about crime does not, in his words, fit the "John Wayne, the Wyatt Earp syndrome." That, by the way, is not the role Humphrey sees for police departments: "Our role is not to usurp the autonomy of the citizens but to let them know that we're willing to work with them as a resource and that if we're going to have an impact on crime and improve the quality of life we must work together."

For anyone living in the first decades of the nineteenth century, Humphrey's description of the relationship between police and community would sound quite familiar. Before police departments were set up in the large eastern seaboard cities, citizens conducted street patrols themselves. Over the ensuing decades police have taken on more and more responsibilities in fighting crime, maintaining order and providing emergency services, but no city can afford to hire enough policemen to handle the patrol or neighborhood watch function as thoroughly as residents themselves will do it—if properly trained and motivated. "The police are singing a much different tune now," said George Kelling, criminologist at Harvard, "but the police have said, 'Leave it up to us. We're crime-fighting professionals, and if you see something, call us, but don't become involved yourself.'"

Police departments that are oriented toward citizen participation and crime prevention are only too eager to provide this training whenever citizens show interest. A department's crime-prevention officer has stacks of folders and brochures on home-security checks, valuables identification, the basics of a neighborhood watch and the telltale signs of crime that citizens should watch out for.

Pittsfield, Massachusetts, an industrial city of 50,000 in the western part of the state, began setting up neighborhood watches in 1979. Burglary rates in the city promptly began falling. The total went from 682 in 1979 down to 547 by 1981, only to zoom back up to 670 in 1982. That recent increase may, according to Detective Edward Sherman, the department's crime-prevention officer, reflect a "false sense of security."

"The neighborhoods thought that just having the neighbor-hood-watch poster up would do it," said Sherman. "Their attitude is 'I'm all set now,' and they go back into their cocoons." In any case, he said the break-ins have not been as frequent in areas that have active watch programs. Burglars, he said, are much like shoplifters. If a would-be shoplifter goes into a store and a clerk, in a helpful but attentive way, makes it clear to him that he will be observed, he won't take the risk. "That's how the neighborhood watch works," said Sherman. "We don't advocate any kind of confrontation. Just let them know that they have been seen." This can mean turning on a porch or outside light, or it can mean writing down the license-plate number of a car whose driver behaves in a way that arouses suspicion.

Sherman cited as an example of the effectiveness of the pro-gram a recent arrest that "cleared" thirty or forty house-breaks on the city's west side. The burglars' method was simplicity itself. They would approach a house, ring the bell and if someone answered ask directions for a nearby address. If no one answered, they would break in. At one house where they asked directions, the man who answered took the trouble, after telling them how to reach their destination, to watch and see if they made the right turn at the end of the street. When they did not, he called the police. The officers reached the scene quickly enough to hear a burglar alarm go off and catch the thieves before they could make a successful getaway. The man who alerted the police need not have been part of a formal program to be as observant as he was. As it happened, though, said Sherman, he had not long before attended one of the police department's meetings on crime pre-vention at a neighborhood school. "A good burglar," said Sherman, "can get past just about any lock or alarm. The one thing he can't avoid is a neighbor's eyes watching him. People have got to become involved. Not paranoid, but suspicious."

In no neighborhood, he said, can a program expect to enroll 100 percent of the residents. A more average figure is 30 or 40 percent. There are just too many people who—if they have not themselves been crime victims—just don't want to be bothered. "The program is always after the fact," he said. Sherman also points out that it isn't just policemen whose self-image sometimes gets in the way of successful crime-prevention work. Often, he said, a male homeowner will reject the notion that he needs help from a police outsider in making his home secure.

As with police crime-fighting, citizen efforts differ from one community to the next. In West Philadelphia, for instance, community organizers noticed that high-crime rates had made residents too fearful to use the streets. So the Citizens Local Alliance for a Safer Philadelphia (CLASP) organized block associations that sponsor "neighborhood walks" at night to reduce this fear of crime.

There is a danger of "burn out" among participants in neighborhood crime programs, a 1982 Ford Foundation information paper observed. A good antidote to that, according to the authors of the Ford report, is to "broaden the scope" of the program's activities to include other problems in the neighborhood besides crime. By the same token, existing block or neighborhood organizations can take on crime-watch responsibilities. Either way, a crime-watch activity stands a better chance of becoming institutionalized if it is part of a broader neighborhood organization, the authors of the Ford report believe.

Televised crime-stopping

One technique that has caught on, especially in the West, is the use of televised reenactments of crimes to jog the memories of witnesses in the community who may not even have known they had been near a crime scene. As an extra inducement for tips, rewards are often offered. Because the informants are often underworld characters themselves or are, for other reasons, wary of becoming involved, the rewards are sometimes paid in the dark of night at secret rendezvous points. While it is a sad commentary on society that many citizens with information on crimes will come forward only for a reward, the police emphasize that many tips come from people who are happy to pass up the monetary gain.

The program began in Albuquerque, where it is called Crime Stoppers, and has since spread to other cities. Typically, it is run by a civilian volunteer board with close contact with the police. Private donations, including many from businesses, defray the costs of rewards and operating expenses. The actors who stage the reenactments are often drama students at local colleges. Crime Stoppers seems to work. In Albuquerque alone, it is credited with solving 1,087 felonies and leading to the recovery of more than $1 million. Rewards granted have totaled less than $100,000—a highly productive investment just on those terms. Televised reenactment of crime for crime-solving purposes was not invented on these shores, by the way. For years, a program of this kind was a popular feature on one of the German TV networks, with the title "The XYZ File." And Crime Stoppers does have its critics. An Albuquerque defense attorney, Leo C. Kelly, warned of the danger of abuse in a 1980 article in *The Wall Street Journal:* "Uncontrolled," he said, "it's a tool that the police can use to buy a witness."

One of the most publicized, and controversial, of all volunteer anticrime groups is the Guardian Angels, which originated in New York City. While police officials often have reservations about patrolling by young people who are not under their direct control, both pedestrians and subway riders in the cities where the Guardian Angels operate have welcomed their presence.

The one major concern voiced about citizen patrols, whether by Guardian Angels or others, is that they will degenerate into vigilantism. So far, this has not become a problem, but the country's history of vigilante excesses stands as a warning that it *could* happen here. Arthur Miller, professor of law at Harvard, points out that Americans have had the historic right of "citizen's arrest," but he advises volunteer patrollers to learn the rules of such arrests in their own jurisdictions.

"People have the right to be on the street, people have the right to protect themselves," Miller said in an ABC interview in February 1983. "So there is no power in the police to prevent these civilian patrols. But as the people in Detroit made very, very clear, it would be very foolish not to work with the police and establish that kind of rapport that makes it more or less two arms of the same team."

In addition to familiarizing themselves with local rules of citizen's arrest, Miller advises volunteers to do the following things: "Establish clear rules of conduct. Know exactly what the group is designed to do—just watch, apprehend, call the police? Third, establish liaison with the police. Fourth, do not drink and do not carry dangerous weapons. And fifth, know the people you go out on the street with. Make sure that they're the kind of people you want to participate in this kind of activity."

For citizens who become involved in nothing more than neighborhood-watch programs—and not actual patrols—these concerns will never arise. For them, the only "drawback" is that they are likely to be thought of as "nosy" by neighbors who choose not to be involved. But that nosiness is one element of the glue that many communities and neighborhoods in this country have lacked. Without it, they are much easier prey to a wide range of criminals, from burglars to sex offenders and muggers. As Pittsfield's Detective Sherman said: "Neighborhood watches don't only cut down on crime, they have a cohesive effect. And cohesiveness is something we haven't had for a long time." The test for these programs will be, as Sherman suggested above, whether they have lasting power if and when crime rates fall in a given area. But if citizens do stick to them, the watches and patrols can bring police and citizens together in ways that make both more effective at preventing and solving crimes. This approach is probably the most promising direct action a community can take to win its streets and neighborhoods back from criminals.

Chapter 7

The "criminal-processing system"

Well, I've always thought it entirely wonderful
that some people can look across the squalor of
the American criminal-justice system from
beginning to end and find the scapegoats in
mollycoddling, sentimental judges. I mean, it's
one of the tributes to the human imagination.
                            —*Norval Morris, University of*
                            Chicago criminologist.

he recent decline in rates of
reported crime in the United States can be counted on to set off a
debate between those who will attribute it almost solely to the fact
that there are fewer young men of the high-crime age in society
and those who will say a good deal of the credit should go to the
sterner sentencing practices of the late 1970s and early 1980s. But
the debate will be conducted more among specialists in the field
than among the public at large which, according to the ABC-News
crime poll, will be surprised to hear that judges have been more
willing to send defendants to prison for longer stretches. According
to the poll, almost two-thirds of those asked thought judges had
been giving shorter sentences in recent years. But, according to a
1981 *Time* magazine survey, the average sentence rose from eighteen
months in 1965 to thirty-five months in 1981.

The predictable debate over reasons behind the decline in the reported-crime rate will echo a longstanding dispute among criminologists and law-enforcement professionals over the capacity of the courts, through their sentencing practices, to affect the incidence of crime. Those who believe courts have little influence over criminals point to the fact that fewer than one in five serious reported crimes is cleared by an arrest. As was mentioned in Chapter 3, most habitual criminals do eventually get caught, but they know fully well that their chances of capture for any individual crime are slight. In his book, *Court Reform on Trial*, Malcolm Feeley writes: "Courts cannot solve the problem of crime or even make a significant dent in it. Thus, in a very real sense the courts—charged with handling society's failures—will always fail. What the family, the church, the workplace and the school cannot do, neither can the courts."

The opposing view is that the courts can do a great deal more than they have done or were doing before the recent increase in incarceration rates. A proponent of this view is James Q. Wilson of Harvard. In his opinion, one has to assume that criminals are "among that small fraction of citizens who are utterly irrational" to contend that their choice of actions will not be affected by the risks associated with it. Wilson refers to studies that, he says, clearly establish that *certainty* of punishment by the criminal courts, if not the *severity* of sentences they impose, has an effect on crime rates. That view is seconded by Whitney North Seymour Jr., a former U.S. attorney in New York. As chairman of the executive committee of Citizens Action on Crime, Seymour wrote an article in 1981 in which he decried "the myth that the criminal-justice system cannot do anything to reduce crime."

Do mandatory sentences reduce crime?

The rejoinder to Wilson's faith in the efficacy of punishment certainty is, of course, that one-in-five figure on the *uncertainty* of arrest for any single crime. Research done for the Justice Department's National Institute of Justice on the deterrent effect of new mandatory-sentencing laws is inconclusive. One study indicated no observable deterrence dividend from a New York law on drug-crime sentencing; another study showed that a Massachusetts mandatory sentence for illegal carrying of a firearm *did* seem to have at least a temporary effect on the use of guns in crimes, although there were signs that publicity about the new law may have had as much impact as the law itself. (All conclusions in this area are necessarily hedged. The methodology of experiments that can prove or disprove a deterrent effect in a new law is an extremely tricky task.) For Feeley, the evidence that mandatory sentences are no panacea does not come as a surprise: "Mandatory sentencing plans failed to increase deterrence because they did not increase arrests. Any reduction of a targeted criminal activity immediately after adoption of new laws was short-lived and was probably due more to a temporary blitz of publicity than to the laws' provisions."

While Seymour speaks of the myth that the courts are helpless in the face of crime, a possibly more dangerous illusion is that courts could be highly instrumental in reducing crime—if they were just operated differently. The illusion is dangerous because it diverts attention from more productive crime-fighting methods and often leads to the passage of laws that hamstring judges in their proper functions and upset the delicate balances that keep undermanned criminal courts from stumbling into the judicial equivalent of gridlock.

It is not difficult, though, to see why the public in its frustration over high crime rates often looks to the judicial system for an answer. Of all the elements of the criminal-justice system, the workings of the courts are the most visible. When the police investigate crimes or make arrests, they are out of the limelight, as are probation and parole officials and corrections officers when they perform their duties. Courts, on the other hand, work under a constitutional requirement to do their business in public. The reader of a newspaper in Chicago will probably not know what criminologists at the University of Chicago discovered when they talked with Chicago police officers: that, for every arrest of a delinquent youth a police officer makes, he will pass up four or five incidents that offer probable cause for arrest. The reader of that newspaper *will* know, however, when a judge in a Chicago criminal court exercises discretion of a different kind and orders a defendant acquitted on grounds of insufficient evidence. That act is public; the police officer's isn't. Discretion is brought to bear throughout the law-enforcement system. It is exercised by police, prosecutors, judges, jurors and parole boards. Only in court is the public invited to watch decisions in the making.

Some of the expectations of courts the public has are not unrealistic. The courts should be institutions of instruction in ethics and justice. They should produce clear, well-founded verdicts and sentences. But the citizens probably ask too much of the judicial system when they expect it, through its verdicts or its sentences, to make major gains in the fight against crime.

Nonetheless, voters have been communicating their distrust of courts and judges to their politicians, and the politicians have responded. Legislatures in several states have passed mandatory-sentence laws. In California, voters used the referendum process to change rules of evidence, restrict use of the insanity defense, change bail standards and forbid plea-bargaining in serious-felony cases. In Massachusetts, there is a move in the legislature to force the state's judges, who are appointed by the governor, to undergo an up-or-down election review every six years. In both Massachusetts and New York, new sentencing proposals would reduce the degree of discretion in the system.

There is nothing new about citizens or politicians grumbling about the alleged leniency of the courts—it has been a campaign-stump standard of politicians going back to the early years of this century, at least. Nor is it surprising that the courts should come under fire now. Reported crime, after all, was on the increase until 1981, and it is still at intolerably high levels. Yet the current criticism of the judiciary on this score of alleged leniency should not be allowed to obscure the fact that the country's courts are operating more professionally, more honestly and more justly than they ever have before. Less politicized selection of court personnel, the right of indigent defendants to counsel at the public's expense, better protection of the defendant's right against self-incrimination, rules on disclosure that open prosecutor files to the defense—all of these reforms in recent decades have helped to make the criminal court a forum where justice is more likely to be done. It would be a shame if any of the interventions into the judicial system under the banner of crime-fighting were to detract from that achievement.

Why cases don't come
to trial

The public's dissatisfaction with the criminal-justice system has a statistical basis in some highly unsettling numbers. As mentioned earlier in this chapter, only a small minority of reported crimes are cleared by an arrest. Of the more than thirteen million Index crimes reported to police in 1981, fewer than one in five—just 19.5 percent—were cleared by an arrest. The clearance rates are much higher for serious crimes (71.6 percent for homicide) and lower for less serious crimes (14.2 percent for auto theft), but the underlying fact is undeniable: Most crimes are not solved.

As if this were not bad enough, the public has also become aware in recent years that, even in cases where arrests are made, the chances are not good that the person arrested will ever be convicted of the offense or spend any time behind bars. In 1979, the police made almost 1.3 million arrests for serious crimes, but "only" 131,047 persons were committed in that year to state or federal prisons. Some offenders were sentenced to county jails, but only one out of ten of those arrested in that year ended up serving "felony" time in a prison. (As it happens, these incarceration rates do not reflect any long-term trend away from tougher sentencing practices. Studies of the disposition of felony cases in the 1920s show similar or lower rates of incarceration.)

The raw figures on how felony arrests deteriorate into dismissals or reductions to misdemeanors make the nation's criminal-justice system resemble nothing so much as one of those antiquated water systems that lose half their water between reservoir and tap. INSLAW has completed a study of case "attrition" in fourteen jurisdictions in 1979. According to its data, for every 100 felony arrests made by police, twenty get screened out almost immediately and thirty are dropped later by prosecutors. Of the fifty that are actually pursued, forty-five defendants plead guilty, four are found guilty after a trial and one is acquitted. Of those forty-nine who are found guilty, either through a plea or a trial, twenty-nine are sentenced either to a jail or a prison.

Is the criminal-justice system—or "criminal-processing" system, in the sardonic phrase of former New York Parole Board Chairman

Edward Hammock—as hapless as these figures make it out to be? Fortunately, the same research organizations that have compiled data on case "attrition," INSLAW and the Vera Institute of Justice in New York, have also studied the patterns and the reasons behind the dismissal or reduction of so many felony charges. From their work, it is apparent that there is far more method than madness in the process.

One fact that quickly became apparent is that in every jurisdiction, prosecutors (and in some cases police) submit felony arrests to a screening process in which they weigh the seriousness of the charge, whether the complainant has had a prior relationship with the accused, the strength of other evidence, the previous record of the accused and the involvement of alcohol or drugs in the incident. Based on this information, the screening official may decide that the case is not worth pursuing or should be reduced to a misdemeanor. His reasoning for this decision can range from a sober assessment that he lacks enough evidence to prove guilt to a belief that the complaining witness will become uncooperative at a later stage.

The unreliability of complaining witnesses who have a prior relationship with the defendant turns out to be one of the major causes behind the dismissal of felony charges. Criminologists have long known that crimes like homicide and rape usually involve victims and perpetrators who are friends, relatives or acquaintances of one another. In recent years, researchers have also discovered a high incidence of prior relationships in crimes that were once thought to be the exclusive province of strangers— robberies and burglaries. According to a Vera Institute study of felony arrests in New York City in the early 1970s, prior relation- ships existed in fully 36 percent of robbery arrests and 39 percent of burglary arrests. It would be wrong, by the way, to conclude from these figures that 36 percent of all robberies and 39 percent of all burglaries in New York involved victims and criminals who knew each other. The percentages referred to above are for robberies and burglaries *cleared by arrests*, and it goes without saying that clearance rates will be higher in such crimes when there is a prior relationship.

In any case, prior relationships are a warning signal to police or prosecutors as they screen cases. The concern of the authorities is that by the time the case goes before a judge, the complaining witness and the defendant will have worked out by themselves whatever disagreement lay behind the accusation of assault, robbery or larceny. As INSLAW points out in its study, at least one jurisdiction, St. Louis, has institutionalized practices designed to assure that victims and witnesses are serious in their determination to pursue charges. In that city, the prosecutor's office has a policy of not reviewing police arrests until the victim and witnesses have been brought to the screening room, interviewed and instructed in the consequences of filing criminal charges. This gives witnesses a chance to back out without placing a further burden on the judicial system.

INSLAW discovered that in five of the seven jurisdictions where it studied why felony charges were dropped, problems with witnesses or evidence were behind at least half the rejections. Witnesses can present difficulties for reasons other than the existence of a prior relationship with the accused. They may have been intoxicated at the time of the crime; they may be derelicts who cannot be counted on to appear for court appointments; they may fear reprisal by the defendant or his friends; or they may themselves be involved in crime and therefore reluctant to help the prosecution.

There are a number of ways that police and prosecutors working together can cut down on the number of felony arrests that never go further than the screening room. Prosecutors could probably make greater efforts to explain to police officers what kind of detail they want in officers' reports and what kind of evidence they would like to see the police providing. Interestingly, INSLAW discovered that in all seven of the jurisdictions where it looked closely at the collapse of cases, a small number of arresting officers accounted for grossly disproportionate percentages of the arrests that ended in convictions. From 8 percent to 19 percent of the officers in each of the seven jurisdictions made 50 percent of the conviction arrests. Moreover, this finding stood up even after such factors as particular officers' assignments were factored out. There are, it is clear, officers in every department who know what prosecutors need to make arrests stick and can provide it. The reliability of witnesses will always be a question mark in felony prosecutions, but better coordination between police and prosecutors would help advance cases that, ideally, should not be dismissed out of hand.

Plea-bargaining

When the ABC-News poll asked people whether criminal cases that they were familiar with came out the way they should have, more than half said no. Much of this dissatisfaction can probably be traced to those forty-five cases out of 100 in which defendants plead guilty. Guilty pleas are often one end of a bargain in which the prosecution agrees to reduce the charge or to recommend a relatively mild sentence. The public doesn't like this plea-bargaining and is often receptive to the campaign pledges of district-attorney candidates who promise to limit it or abolish it altogether. In 1982, California voters chose to forbid plea-bargaining in serious-felony cases when they approved Proposition 8.

The standard criticisms of plea-bargaining are that it lets defendants off with sentences lighter than they deserve and, perhaps more important, that it coerces defendants into forfeiting their right to a trial. The standard defense of it is that it is a necessary evil. Without it, the argument goes, an unmanageable number of defendants would ask for full trials and would tie an already overworked and underfunded judicial system into knots.

Whatever the merits of these two positions, the arguments reflect an assumption that plea-bargaining is a relatively recent phenomenon in American courts and that it is used primarily in high-traffic, big-city courts, while less congested courts settle proportionately more cases through trials. Both of these assumptions are off base.

A study of Connecticut courts by Milton Heumann showed that from 1880 to 1954 there was an almost constant ratio of one trial conviction for every ten guilty dispositions, with the rest pleas. Moreover, Heumann found that this ratio held true through those decades in both high-volume and low-volume courts. In the 1920s, Raymond Moley, who later became part of Franklin Roosevelt's brain trust and then a fierce FDR critic, studied New York State's courts and found that in the early years of this century about 90 percent of all cases ended in pleas, with the percentage even higher in rural areas than in cities. These findings have been backed up by the research of legal historians in other areas. As the INSLAW study points out, the one-to-ten ratio that keeps reappearing "is virtually the same as that calculated in [its] report" for present-day courts.

If there was a period in U.S. history when criminal cases were resolved primarily by trials, it was before the Civil War and it may even have been in the eighteenth century. But whenever the golden age of adversarial proceedings was, there was probably little luster to it. In *Court Reform on Trial*, Malcolm Feeley describes what trials must have been like at a time when one court would handle six or more cases in a single day: "Typically, the prosecutor would summarize the charges and introduce the complaining witness, who would tell his or her story quickly. Usually, defendants who were unrepresented by counsel remained silent or stammered a sentence or two of defense. After a brief deliberation, the jury would give its verdict, and if the verdict was guilty the judge would immediately pronounce sentence. The few rules of evidence and procedure were usually honored in the breach."

Although it will come as a surprise to many that plea convictions have predominated in the nation's courts for the past 130 years at least, it's not all that unreasonable. A trial is called for when there are matters of fact to be decided, but in the vast majority of criminal cases that make it through that initial screening process there are usually few crucial facts to be contested. In many cases, the "negotiation" that occurs between prosecution and defense is distinctly one-sided, with the prosecutor under no pressure to make concessions. Feeley has characterized plea negotiations that he witnessed in a New Haven, Connecticut, court as being in the nature of informational discussions in which the two sides discussed the facts of the case to arrive at an agreement on what crime was actually committed. Once that agreement is reached, the penalty is usually self-evident. Outright granting of concessions, he found, was more the exception than the rule. Other observers have noticed a greater frequency of concession-granting in big-city courts, but it is clear that not every plea represents a "deal" as such.

The fear of losing

The high incidence of pleas in courts that do not face overwhelming criminal dockets is strong evidence of the logic of plea convictions, even in jurisdictions where prosecutors do not feel inordinate pressure to keep the judicial assembly line moving. One factor in this phenomenon has to do with the competitive nature of the legal profession. Lawyers—both defense attorneys and prosecutors—may not be driven to win every case, but they don't like to lose in trial. Prosecutors, especially elected ones, keep a "batting average" of convictions versus acquittals that usually doesn't differentiate between plea convictions and trial convictions—an infield single is as good as a line drive off the outfield wall. Trials introduce an element of risk that neither side can control. Even lawyers who consider the jury system as sacred as anything handed down from the Mount have horror stories that illustrate the total unpredictability of twelve sworn jurors.

Defense attorneys have a special concern about trials. In a case in which their client's guilt is largely a foregone conclusion, the attorney has to worry about the effect that a detailed recitation of the evidence by victims and witnesses will have on the judge's (in some jurisdictions, jury's) sentencing decision. In a plea conviction, the judge is likely to hear only the prosecutor's more matter-of-fact summary of the evidence.

Proof of lawyers' wariness with regard to trials can be found on the civil side of the judicial system as well as on the criminal side. Here, too, the percentage of cases resolved by a negotiated settlement greatly exceeds the share that actually go to trial. "A fear of losing," in one lawyer's phrase, creates a bias against trials throughout the system.

This does not mean that trials do not play an important role in American criminal courts. The 10 percent of cases resolved this way set the standards for the 90 percent that end in pleas. Defense attorneys and prosecutors watch the trials for what they indicate about current interpretation of rules of evidence and procedure, sentencing trends and other factors that then become the spoken or unspoken ground rules of plea negotiations.

Admittedly, there are abuses in the system. In many cases in which the crassest kind of bargaining occurs, the prosecutor knows that his own case has a flaw that will make it difficult to sustain the original charge in an actual trial. In those circumstances, he does have an incentive to bargain and may agree to a reduced charge and a light sentence. From the outside, this resolution may look like lenient treatment, but it could well be the only way the prosecution can secure a conviction and get the defendant to serve any time at all.

ABC News focused its cameras on just such a case in a Texas court. One Leo Joseph Butler was accused of the second-degree felony offense of attempted murder for having choked an elderly woman on July 29, 1982. After a negotiation between Butler's attorney and the prosecutor, Butler agreed to plead guilty to the offense and to accept a nineteen-year prison sentence. The alternative for the defendant, who had already served time in prison for rape, was a trial in which he could be found guilty and sentenced to life in prison.

On the face of it, Butler seems to have gotten the better of the deal. What he and his attorney did not know, however, was that the assistant district attorney in the case knew that the victim would not testify against the defendant. Without that testimony, the prosecution could have lost the case altogether in a trial. And, as the assistant district attorney pointed out to an ABC correspondent, since Butler pleaded for nineteen years with no appeal, it was "an opportunity to take him off the streets today." One might argue that a case like this, with a recalcitrant crucial witness, should have been dropped at an earlier stage. But given the seriousness of the charge and the defendant's previous record, that would have been a difficult decision for a prosecutor to make.

The manipulators

Clearly, plea-bargaining has much to recommend it. It serves the purposes of lawyers and "the system," and it often moderates what would otherwise be excessive or arbitrary sentences. And while there are the dangers that bargaining encourages prosecutors to "overcharge" defendants in anticipation of later deals and that it leads innocent defendants to forfeit their right to trial in exchange for light sentences, these problems can probably be minimized.

Much of the unease that plea-bargaining arouses among members of the public and professionals in the criminal-justice system is its furtiveness and the possibilities of abuse it creates on the part of the prosecutors, defense attorneys and defendants. In

1967, the President's Commission on Law Enforcement and the Administration of Justice discussed this issue in terms that are just as relevant today: "Cutting across the entire system of plea negotiation is the fear that the low visibility of the proceeding lends itself to possible corrupt manipulation. In actual practice such corruption seems rare. But a real vice in the procedure may be that it often gives the defendant an image of corruption in the system, or at least an image of a system lacking meaningful purpose and subject to manipulation by those who are wise to the right tricks. Cynicism, rather than respect, is the likely result."

This is an important consideration. If the judicial system is to encourage citizens to be law-abiding, it does so, in large part, by encouraging respect for a system of laws in general. If that respect is damaged among those citizens who are brought into the system as defendants or witnesses, it is difficult to imagine how even quite stringent sentencing practices can do much to reestablish the validity and credibility of laws and the criminal-justice system.

One frequent defense made of plea-bargaining is—and this can be demonstrated statistically—that it is used much less often in cases of serious offenses or for defendants who have previous records. By the same token, however, this means that plea-bargaining is used *more* often in the cases of defendants coming into the system for the first or second time, with still unformed impressions about criminal justice. As limited as the judicial system's capacity is to have a significant effect in correcting society's failures, that capacity is reduced further if still-impressionable first offenders' experience with the system teaches them that it operates by wheeling and dealing and does not take their crimes very seriously.

Rufus Saunders, the convicted robber from Brooklyn, New York, described to ABC News his reaction after his first arrest and prompt release: "I was very scared my first arrest, but going into a courthouse setting and being in the bullpens with other people that's arrested, you can't show a fear . . . But I was afraid. I was afraid because I didn't know what this was all about, the gates are slamming. I want to yell out, 'Where's my mother? Where's my father?' . . . And when I went before the judge and he released me, that fear I had just went away. It just went away. You know, all that I thought in the bullpen, in terms of 'I'm never going to do this again' . . . But once he released me, that was gone. And it was gone. It's back to the corner and back to the fellows."

Even after a subsequent offense, Saunders was able to have a serious armed robbery charge reduced to a lesser felony that got him a two-to-four-year sentence. "Through plea-bargaining and patience I wound up with two to four years," he said. "Two to four, I mean that was a joke."

Can the system function without plea-bargaining? Many of those who work in the system say it couldn't. "What else are we to do?" asked Judge Pat Lykos of Harris County, Texas, when the question was posed to her in an ABC-News interview. "Unless we just absolutely drown and the whole system, to mix a metaphor, comes to a halt."

When an ABC correspondent asked Judge Ricardo Torres of the Los Angeles Superior Court what he thought the effect of California's just-passed ban on plea-bargaining in serious felony cases would be, he said, "I think that it will cause the courts to logjam over the long run... Nobody wants to plead guilty to a case unless he knows what reward he's getting for pleading guilty. If he's going to receive exactly the same thing, why should he plead guilty? He could take his chances and go to trial. Maybe something will go wrong in the prosecution's case."

These contentions that an end to plea-bargaining would cause courts to be swamped with trials they could not handle without enormously increased manpower have been challenged by the state of Alaska's now eight-year-old experiment in operating without negotiated pleas. In 1975, the state's attorney general issued a flat ban on the practice for both felony and misdemeanor cases. In the beginning, some prosecutors circumvented the ban by engaging in charge-bargaining, as opposed to sentence-bargaining, and some judges made sentence commitments of their own to defendants, a practice which the state's highest court then explicitly prohibited. But by 1978 and 1979, according to an evaluation of the Alaskan experience funded by the National Institute of Justice, explicit bargaining had come to almost a total halt.

Contrary to expectations, the new rules did not throw Alaska's criminal-justice system into disarray. At the same time the ban was introduced, a number of administrative reforms were also made, and the time span between arrest and disposition actually fell. There was an increase in trials, but it was not overwhelming. Before 1975, 10 percent of convictions had come after trial; after the ban, that rose to 19 percent. The average annual number of trials in the state's three largest cities rose from 110 to 149, an increase that, in the words of INSLAW's summary of the Alaska experience, does not "sound sufficiently large to create an administrative nightmare." Research indicated that sentences imposed after trials did tend to be slightly longer on average than those imposed after pleas, but this was also the case before bargaining was eliminated. Moreover, the INSLAW study of felony arrests points out, it is impossible to tell whether the discrepancy in sentencing severity between plea convictions and trial convictions is attributable to that fact or to differences in the details of the cases or the defendants' records.

Alaska may be a special case, however. Previous attempts to eliminate sentencing-bargaining have simply shoved it into other areas. During one city's experience with a ban on bargaining, prosecutors made sentencing concessions to defendants who waived their right to a jury trial and instead chose a quick "bench" trial before a judge. A more reliable test of whether plea-bargaining is a necessary expedient in high-volume criminal courts will come from California's Proposition 8 experiment. If past experience is any guide, the first reports on that state's experience should not be taken as final.

Other states will undoubtedly observe how the situation develops in California and if a no-bargaining rule seems workable without a great addition in resources for the judicial system, some will try it. Another alternative that has been tried in some jurisdictions has been to exert more judicial control over plea-bargaining or to formalize and regulate it in other ways. In some jurisdictions, prosecutors hold pretrial conferences with, in many cases, the defendant, victim and arresting officer. In *Criminal Violence, Criminal Justice*, Charles Silberman describes the "dignified, if informal" proceedings of such conferences in the Detroit prosecutor's office. Pleas are negotiated but with more uniformity than is often the case and with the knowledge of the victim and arresting officer. "Prosecutorial decisions," Silberman writes, "that otherwise might appear arbitrary become comprehensible; this, in turn, shores up the legitimacy of the system."

Whatever rules on plea-bargaining a particular state or city adopts, an important test is whether or not the process does, in fact, "shore up the legitimacy of the system." The goal should be to end the situation described to ABC by Michael Genelin, a deputy district attorney in Los Angeles: "These people are manipulators. They've manipulated the system before, and they know that the system can be manipulated further. So they play games in the system itself."

Punishment to fit the crime

Laws that abolish or restrict plea-bargaining are an attempt to limit the immense discretion that prosecutors have in the American criminal-justice system; mandatory sentencing laws are an attempt to tie the hands not only of prosecutors but of judges and parole authorities as well. Such laws are not newcomers on the American scene. It was only in this century that judges (and parole boards) were granted the broad discretion of "indeterminate" sentences and wide use of probation. Even during the height of this trend, legislatures from time to time passed mandatory minimums for particular offenses—often to see them evaded by prosecutors or judges.

The vogue of wide discretion in sentencing was informed by a belief that prison could be or should be a rehabilitative experience for the offender. From this point of view, the length of a sentence should be determined less by the seriousness of the crime than by the inmate's progress in ridding himself of the antisocial tendencies that got him into trouble. As it happened, even in such states as California, which institutionalized the "indeterminate" sentence most formally, actual terms served tended to reflect the seriousness of the crime and the offender's past record more than any perceived rehabilitation. Rehabilitation was the rationale of the sentencing system—it was never really its operating principle.

In the last decade and a half, rehabilitation as even a theory of sentencing has lost much of its credibility. No prison rehabilitation program by itself has been demonstrated to be especially successful in getting offenders to go straight. Most offenders straighten out eventually, it appears, as part of the aging process. Marriage, family responsibilities, a distaste for further incarceration—these seem to be the crucial factors in making law-abiding citizens out of lawbreakers. "Marriage and the family," Charles Silberman wrote in *Criminal Violence, Criminal Justice,* "are the most effective correctional institutions we have."

A further criticism of basing the sentencing practices on a judge's or parole board's hunch about an offender's rehabilitation is that it can lead to grossly unfair results. If rehabilitation is the theoretical goal of a sentencing system, few white-collar criminals would ever go to jail. The ignominy of an arrest and conviction would usually be enough to keep them from ever again fixing prices or plotting Watergates. Even in the case of a violent crime, a white, middle-aged defendant with a family, job and no drug habit will—under a strictly rehabilitative sentencing code—get off much more lightly than a young black who committed the same crime but had no family, no job and a serious drug problem. In California, inmates were dissatisfied with the state's "indeterminate" sentencing because it left them in such uncertainty as to when they would be released.

That uncertainty existed in California prisons for each individual prisoner. Across the board, as Feeley points out, the terms served were quite predictable and "only a handful of offenders actually served their maximum terms or had their terms determined as a result of treatment and rehabilitation." The release-granting authority, Feeley writes, "usually followed a well-established practice that translated the law's indeterminate sentences into a more or less fixed fraction of the maximum sentence allowable."

In any case, by the 1960s and 1970s, states turned away from this rehabilitative ideal in the theory as well as the practice of their sentencing. Other goals for sentencing were given new emphasis. In one view, prison or jail sentences, even if brief, should be relied on more as a deterrent to crime. This became an argument for mandatory minimum sentence. In another, related view, heavier use of prison sentences would—even if it did not deter criminals— at least keep lawbreakers from committing additional offenses for the length of their prison stays. In practice, this approach means throwing the book at repeat offenders or other criminals who, in the opinion of the authorities, show a high likelihood of dangerousness.

A third position was that sentencing should be based less on an imagined benefit of deterrence or a prediction of likely danger- ousness and more simply on the seriousness of the crime, with some allowance for consideration of the offender's previous record. This is the "just deserts" or "commensurate deserts" principle of punishment. Andrew von Hirsch, a Rutgers University criminologist and author of *Doing Justice*, described this approach in an ABC-News interview: "Punishment is an instrument of condemnation, and if somebody does something that's very blameworthy, that's very serious, he ought to be given a good dose of condemnation, and the way to do that is to impose a substantial sentence."

All of the new approaches to sentencing would, to some extent, reduce the discretion that is now exercised—some would say abused—by judges and parole boards. Sentencing standards or guidelines would be set by legislatures or judicial sentencing boards or would be maintained indirectly by appellate review. Whichever approach is taken, if the codes imposed severely limit the courts' ability to tailor sentences to individual circumstances, they run the risk of fostering greater reliance by courts on pretrial plea-bargaining over charges. "You're going to have discretion as a given in the criminal-justice system," argued Harvard law professor Alan Dershowitz in an ABC-News interview. "The question is whether we channel it, whether we focus it, whether we hold people responsible for exercising it, or whether we let it creep in in undetermined ways throughout the system, in ways that we can't control."

Another obvious cost in most of the tougher sentencing systems is that they require the building of new prison capacity and the hiring of new corrections personnel. While more than three-quarters of those questioned in the ABC-News poll expressed a willingness to support new prison construction as a crime-fighting measure, voters have been less enthusiastic when put to the test. The record for prison-construction bond issues in the past few years has been mixed, at best.

Selective incapacitation

The financial constraint on tough sentencing practices unquestionably accounts for the appeal of a sentencing technique known as selective incapacitation. Selective incapacitation, its proponents say, offers a more cost-effective way of isolating a high percentage of the criminals who are committing the most crimes. By using a profile based on an offender's known

prior record (including juvenile record) and his recent employment and drug-abuse history, a sentencing judge can, in theory,
predict which convicted persons should get long sentences and
which should get relatively light ones. One such profile was put
together by Peter Greenwood, a Rand Corporation researcher in
the criminal-justice field.

"The idea of selective incapacitation," Greenwood told ABC,
"is you want to take these high-rate robbers, the ones who do thirty
or forty a year, lock those up for longer terms; and we take these
other offenders who only do one or two crimes a year, and to make
room for the high-rate offenders, we give these low-risk offenders
short terms."

One obvious hitch in this, which Greenwood readily admits, is
that determining high-rate robbers by a profile that includes
factors like employment history is a highly fallible guide. Typically,
criminologists say, prediction methods of this kind cast too wide a
net—many offenders who would not turn out to be high-rate
robbers would be fingered by the Greenwood profile. At the same
time, the profile would fail to identify a fairly substantial percentage of offenders who would, over time, become high-rate
criminals. As von Hirsch points out, these failures would create
political pressure to broaden the sweep of the profile, which would
only increase the number of falsely identified high-rate offenders
as well as the total number of persons incarcerated. The less
selective the system becomes, the more society has to spend on
prisons. Von Hirsch also points out that the crime-reduction
potential of selective incapacitation is greatly reduced if the high-
crime individuals it nominates for long imprisonment are members
of gangs who are simply replaced by new recruits. Because of these
problems and others that von Hirsch and others have drawn
attention to, a state that systematically used Greenwood's selective-
incapacitation methods might find that its efforts have not produced
the crime-rate reduction that Greenwood promises.

Except for the more sophisticated profile that it uses, Greenwood's
selective incapacitation approach is actually not much different
from other sentencing systems that give the longest sentences to
repeat offenders. Dershowitz called it "old wine in an old bottle
with a new label and a new vintage."

"If we could figure out who the people are who commit tomorrow's crimes and next week's crimes," Dershowitz said, "obviously nobody would object to keeping them in jail, especially if they've already committed a crime which justifies them being kept in jail. The problem is we don't have a crystal ball."

Mandatory or presumptive sentences?

One sentencing reform that cost a great deal without causing any noticeable diminution of the crime it was aimed at was the late Governor Nelson Rockefeller's program of mandatory narcotics-offense sentences in New York State. Instituted in 1973, the major parts of the law were finally repealed in 1979 but not before the state had to shell out more than $40 million a year in salaries alone and additional millions in new capital costs, according to Feeley in *Court Reform on Trial.* His summary of that law should make other state legislatures think twice before an ambitious politician tries to put through sweeping new mandatory sentences: "To its credit, the legislature [in 1979] acknowledged that the critics had been correct; the law had little measurable deterrent effect on narcotics use, it was astronomically expensive to administer, and it led to harsh sentences for marginal offenders and little increase in punishment for major offenders."

Dershowitz is an advocate of what is known as "presumptive" sentencing. Less restrictive than mandatory sentencing, a presumptive code sets a standard sentence based on the seriousness of the offense and the offender's record of past convictions and then allows the judge to deviate from that standard if circumstances justify it. To make such a deviation, however, a judge has to write an opinion justifying it. Dershowitz sees presumptive sentencing as a middle ground between the extreme of discretion permitted under indeterminate sentencing and the lack of discretion permitted with mandatory sentences. Minnesota has instituted such a system in its courts. Its experience will be followed to see if it avoids the pitfalls of too much or too little discretion.

In considering any sentencing system, the caution expressed by von Hirsch in an ABC interview is in order: "I think the idea that if we only do this we're going to stop crime—that there's some sort of silver bullet out there that we can use to stop criminal activity—that, I think, is not the case. I think what we can do is make the system fairer, and part of really making it fairer is to be fairly severe when people commit very, very serious crimes."

The most severe sentence of all, the death penalty, is on the books in thirty-eight states, even though there has never been solid evidence that it deters crime. Another argument for capital punishment—that it serves a "just deserts" function for anyone who commits a heinous offense—also does not stand up well under experience. Since 1976, when the U.S. Supreme Court ruled that carefully drawn death-penalty statutes do not necessarily violate the Eighth Amendment's prohibition against "cruel and unusual" punishment, about 1,200 men and women have been sentenced to death, but only a handful have been executed—and four of them gave up their appeals and asked to be put to death.

The passage of capital-punishment laws suggests a strong faith on the part of the public in the criminal-justice system's ability to avoid the kind of mistake that in the case of the death penalty is of course irrevocable. This expression of faith is paradoxical because the public is indicating in numerous other ways that it has relatively little faith in the system. At bottom, it may simply be that the public is not terribly concerned about mistakes in imposing the death sentence or is reassured by the panoply of due-process and appeal rights that are available to the offender.

Those rights are what has kept all of those condemned persons on Death Row alive for years after their convictions. By trying to make this penalty as error-free as possible, the system has made it unusual, indeed. But the discrepancy between more than 100,000 arrests for homicide since 1976 and so few executions may be the criminal-justice system's way of making another point about the death penalty. As this book has endeavored to make clear, that system relies on a high quantum of discretion to do justice. In many of the most serious offenses, successful prosecution of a case requires the striking of a deal between a prosecutor and a perpetrator as a way of securing evidence against co-defendants. In a capital case that requires this kind of cooperation with a defendant, it isn't just the prosecutor, judge and juries who will be playing God with someone's life—a criminal will, too. It is not surprising that Americans show more enthusiasm for passing death-penalty laws than for actually carrying through executions.

One of the most simply stated arguments against capital punishment was made by Norval Morris in *The Honest Politician's Guide to Crime Control*: "The question is, Will people learn to respect life better by threat or by example? And the uniform answer of history, comparative studies and experience is that man is an emulative animal."

prison cell

Chapter 8

Leaving "room for reform" in prisons

There are all sorts of reasons why people give up crime. But very few people, to our knowledge, quit because they've been put into some counseling program while in the prison or one in the probation · services. And it's not that nothing works, but, not very much works very well.

—Andrew von Hirsch,
Rutgers University criminologist.

or all the differences in the states' sentencing systems, the result across the nation is much the same: More and more offenders are going to prison. This is true in states with presumptive sentencing, mandatory sentencing, indeterminate sentencing. Of the fifty states, the only one that did not see an increase in inmates in 1981 was Michigan—it released prisoners under a new emergency "rollback" law that requires the discharging of prisoners when the census reaches a limit and new offenders are brought into the system.

The greater willingness of judges to sentence offenders to prison—and to set longer sentences—is evident in states that have traditionally had low incarceration rates and in states that have always had a relatively high inmate population. Utah, whose incarceration rate is just half the national average, saw its figure jump by 22.3 percent in 1981. In Georgia, which has one of the highest rates of imprisonment, the population behind bars grew by 14.9 percent. Nationally, the prison population went up 12.1 percent in 1981, 11.6 percent in 1982. Of the nine states whose inmate populations grew by 20 percent or more in 1981, five were already among the more than thirty that are under court orders to reduce overcrowding.

Actual increases in crime are certainly a factor in the rising incarceration rates, but the increases in the latter have far outstripped either the increases in the FBI's total of reported crimes or the increases in the number of arrests made. One phenomenon that is a definite factor in the bulging inmate population is the reduced faith in parole—the release under supervision of an offender before his formal term is completed—in many states. Maine, for example, is one of seven states that have done away with parole altogether. Since that step was taken in Maine five years ago, the average prison stay has doubled. In many states that have not actually eliminated parole, its use is severely restricted.

As a result of these pressures for more and longer prison sentences, the total state and federal prison population grew in 1982 by 42,915—the largest one-year growth in history. Today, the nationwide prison population is more than 400,000. One out of 600 Americans is an inmate, an incarceration rate that is matched by only the Soviet Union and the Union of South Africa.

Unfortunately, states are not building cells as fast as they are increasing their inmate populations. According to *Overcrowded Time*, a publication of the Edna McConnell Clark Foundation, in 1981 new housing was built or under construction for just four out of ten of the new inmates. Prison overcrowding is almost as old as the penal technique of imprisonment itself. Michigan's technique of simply discharging prisoners whenever numbers reach a certain limit (a technique that several other states employ as well) was used by governors going back into the early years of the nineteenth century. As Malcolm M. Feeley points out in *Court Reform on Trial*, the practice of controlling inmate behavior by offering early release for "good time" also stems from this early era in American penology. New York, Feeley writes, passed the first good-time law in 1817; by 1869 such laws were on the books in most states. In recent years, reduced use of good time, like the new limits on parole, has both increased inmate populations and contributed to tensions within prison walls.

Doubts about rehabilitation

The Justice Department's Bureau of Justice Statistics keeps annual data on state and federal prisoners and publishes a graph of the rise in their numbers over the decades. From 1925 until the mid-1970s, the trend was a steady but not steep increase, with decreases occurring only during World War II and the 1960s. The prisoner population began rising at a much faster rate, however, in the mid-1970s. That change coincided with the publication in 1974 of a report by the late Robert Martinson, a criminologist who evaluated 231 studies of corrections programs inside and outside of prisons and came to an unequivocal conclusion: "With few and isolated exceptions, the rehabilitative efforts that have been reported so far have had no appreciable effect on recidivism."

The Martinson report was the most carefully researched expression of a growing consensus in criminology that attempts at rehabilitating offenders may serve some purposes, but they do not have much effect on that seemingly incorrigible minority of prisoners who do not stay out of trouble after their first prison term. It is, by the way, a minority. Nationally, three out of four prisoners out on parole do not violate their parole terms; in New York, the success rate of parolees is 92 percent. (Interpreting recidivism rates is tricky. If the only measure of backsliding in former convicts is the number who are returned to prison, this figure probably underestimates actual recidivism, since there is plainly a certain number who get into scrapes that go undetected or that are deemed not sufficiently important to justify revocation of parole.)

In any case, the phenomenon of the hard-core recidivist shows up in programs as well designed as the data-processing company run for inmates at Minnesota's Stillwater maximum-security prison. The only private business run entirely within the walls of a prison, Stillwater Data Processing Systems Incorporated pays up to $7 an hour to inmates who work as computer programmers on contracts for such big Minnesota firms as Honeywell, 3M and Pillsbury. But even with the superb background that Stillwater Data provides, five of the seventeen inmate "graduates" of the program were returned to prison after their release.

The recognized failure of prison rehabilitation programs to make a substantial dent in the recidivism rate of released prisoners has forced state legislators and officials throughout the criminal-justice system to reexamine the rationale of punishment. As was pointed out in the chapter before this one, rehabilitation was always more a theoretical than a practical basis for punishment, but the doubt cast on its efficacy has led lawmakers, prosecutors and judges to think of sentences more than ever as a way to deter criminals and to protect the public by getting a convicted criminal off the streets for an extended period of time.

In some cases, the trend to longer sentences actually predated a state's formal adoption of a more stringent sentencing code. California prison censuses, for instance, started rising in 1978, the year *before* the state switched from indeterminate sentences to determinate ones. The trend toward more severe sentencing was described in an ABC-News interview by Walter Lewis, a deputy district attorney in Los Angeles: "It's toughened up considerably in the last few years not only because of Proposition 8 [the new California law forbidding plea-bargaining in serious-felony cases] but because of other forces. The criminal-justice system has always been, up until a few years ago, a closed club, and the club is opening up. The media are taking a look at it and because of that . . . we're getting tougher. Judges are getting tougher. The laws are getting tougher. D.A.s are getting tougher, and people are going to prison for longer periods of time."

A "constructive work program"

Even though few criminologists have much faith in the capacity of rehabilitation programs to affect recidivism rates, the better-run prisons still try to offer jobs, vocational training and classroom instruction—if only to reduce the idleness and boredom of prison life that is so often a cause of unrest or rioting. Another advantage of programs of this kind is that they bring outsiders into prisons, making the community more aware of what goes on behind walls. Moreover, as David C. Anderson, former editor of Criminal Justice Publications, points out, rehabilitative programs help to attract to prison staffs better-educated personnel with a sense of professionalism and not just a bent for authoritarianism.

In a March 1983 article in *Across the Board,* Anderson wrote: "Most of the practitioners now agree that rehabilitation is not necessarily something an institution can impose on an individual. But they also believe, and can cite case after case in support of their belief, that [rehabilitation] is very possible when the individual decides to change himself, and that when an individual does so, it is the obligation of the prison to offer him as much help as possible."

Virtually every prison official that ABC correspondents interviewed made this same point: Correctional institutions should at least, in criminologist Franklin E. Zimring's phrase, "leave room for reform." Or, as George Sumner, the warden of Nevada State Prison put it, "I'm not very liberal and I don't want to sound like a do-gooder, but I think it's important to have a constructive work program. Ninety-something percent of those inmates are going to come back into the community some day, sooner or later, so let's prepare them to succeed when they come back."

Unfortunately, all too few prisons have either the facilities or the personnel to leave room for reform. Prison classes, vocational or academic, often have long waiting lists; prison industries are woefully inadequate for the task. According to *Overcrowded Time,* prisons have jobs for just 10 percent of their inmates. To make matters worse, many of the jobs that are available are field-labor work or shop work with outmoded equipment, neither of which is much preparation for the urban scene to which most inmates return. An inmate at Nevada State Prison described to ABC interviewers how the purposelessness of prison existence can make offenders unfit for life on the outside: "If you're used to working fifteen minutes a day, getting up when you want, doing what you want the rest of the day, it's infeasible to expect you to go out there and work eight hours a day. You cannot give that to an employer."

Rehabilitation programs were never universal in U.S. prisons; they have become even more difficult to operate under the conditions of overcrowding that are now so common. Prison officials have to place their first priority on maintaining physical control of their institutions. "At the most crowded prisons," *Overcrowded*

Time states, "there is real question as to whether the staff controls any more than the walls and barbed-wire fences that keep the inmates from escaping."

To make maximum use of space and to save money on new construction, more and more states are making use of dormitories, as opposed to cells, for housing their inmates. According to *Over-crowded Time*, in 1978, 40 percent of all prisoners were living in dormitories, which foster even more violence and stress than cellblock life. Not infrequently, that publication states, prison guards are afraid to enter dormitories, so intimidated are they by the inmates who greatly outnumber them in the rooms.

"The more crowded it gets," Kenneth McKinney, a Nevada corrections officer, told ABC News, "the more dangerous it gets. The inmates, their stress builds because they have no release area. The more stress they have, the more stress it causes on the officers."

Overcrowding's fatal toll

In January 1980, New Mexico prison officials received an explicit warning from a visiting corrections official from another state that they were "playing Russian roulette with the lives of inmates, staff and the public" at the overcrowded New Mexico State Penitentiary in Santa Fe, which had been the target of an American Civil Liberties Union suit in 1978 for overcrowding. Two weeks after the warning, prisoners set off one of the bloodiest prison riots in the nation's history. Thirty-three inmates died, some in fires and through drug overdoses but most at the hands of other inmates, and five guards were severely beaten. While that was the worst recent incident of prison violence, smaller outbreaks and a much higher rate of inmate suicide and murder have become a depressingly common feature of prison life at institutions all over the country.

This is the reality of life in the overcrowded jails and prisons of the United States in the 1980s: gang warfare, homosexual rapes, stabbings, occasional riots, very little in the way of constructive programs. Conditions have deteriorated to this point because governors, legislators and, most basically, voters have been unwilling to back up their get-tough attitudes on sentencing with support for the new prison capacity that frequent and long sentences necessitate. The cost is formidable. While it is possible to build new facilities on the cheap for $35,000 a cell or so, a mid-range figure is more than $50,000, and the new, state-of-the-art facility in Minnesota carried a price tag of $78,300 per cell.

Beyond that, it costs about $15,000 to feed and guard an inmate for a year. Both capital and operating costs increase as institutions attempt to operate rehabilitative programs. Under those circumstances, the per-capita operating cost can go as high as $30,000 a year. The United States is now spending about $5 billion a year on prisons; by one estimate, it would cost an additional $8 billion to $10 billion just to build all the cells that are needed to provide a minimally acceptable amount of space for the inmates who are now in custody.

This massive undertaking of construction and staffing would be more feasible if the fiscal situation of state governments were better. But, as a spring 1983 publication of the National Governors Association states: "The fiscal condition of the states is the bleakest in recent memory. State after state has been forced to cut programs, enact new taxes, or both. Even so, unless further actions are taken, the aggregate state budget deficit for fiscal 1983 is estimated to be nearly $4 billion." It is questionable whether the states would make the investment needed in new prison facilities if they had the money; with the money not readily available, the issue simply goes unmentioned in many legislative sessions. Arthur Miller, a Harvard law professor, was skeptical in an ABC interview about society's readiness to pay the cost of a corrections system that would be adequate for current sentencing practices: "Legislatures are just unwilling to spend the money to build new prisons or to repair the ones we've got. And, let's face it, people don't care. They don't even want to know what goes on behind these fences."

That opinion may be slightly overdrawn. In 1982, voters in California, Florida and New Jersey did approve bond issues for jail or prison construction. Only in Rhode Island did such a bond issue fail. The situation would be a good deal more encouraging, though, if such bond issues—or straight legislative approvals of prison-construction proposals—were more common than they are.

*Cruel and
unusual punishment
in U.S. prisons?*

In the opinion of many corrections experts, future improvements in prison conditions (like ones of the recent past) are as likely to come from court decisions as from any actions by legislatures. In the past decade, judges have breathed new life into the Eighth Amendment's ban on "cruel and unusual punishment." Prisons in thirty-seven states are under court orders or consent decrees to improve conditions, most often by reducing overcrowding.

In 1981, in *Rhodes v. Chapman*, the U.S. Supreme Court took what seemed to many to be a step away from federal-court intervention into state prison situations when it declared that double-celling (in a cell originally built for one inmate) in an Ohio prison was *not* a violation of the Eighth Amendment. As it happens, however, the institution in *Rhodes* was new and considered to be a model facility, with high-quality medical care, library resources, sanitation and food. There was no evidence, Justice Lewis F. Powell, Jr., noted in his decision for the majority, that double-celling had caused any violence or a high degree of unrest among the inmates. These factors clearly weighed heavily in the majority decision not to rule against double-celling in that instance.

It may not take long, however, for an Eighth Amendment case involving a much less ideal prison to reach the court. Just five months after the *Rhodes* decision, a federal district court in Illinois ruled that double-celling in that state's Pontiac State Prison *was* unconstitutional. The decision specifically contrasted conditions at Pontiac with those at the Ohio prison: "Pontiac is overcrowded, antiquated and has inadequate facilities . . . The confinement for years on end of two adult males . . . in a cramped, ill-ventilated, noisy space . . . is contrary to every recognized penalty . . . and constitutes cruel and unusual punishment."

As the federal courts tackle these "one-man, one-cell" cases, they are gradually setting standards of minimum square-footage per inmate, for both dormitory and cell situations. The American Medical Association, the American Correctional Association and the American Public Health Association all recommend a minimum of sixty square feet. According to figures published by the U.S. Justice Department, fewer than one-third of the nation's prisons now provide this much space per inmate. It seems likely that, sooner or later, many states are going to find themselves required either to send fewer offenders to prison for less time or else spend unprecedented amounts of money on the incarceration of their inmate populations. An additional factor in this difficult decision-making is that crime rates are already beginning to decline, with the fall-off in numbers among the most crime-prone segment of the population. If incarceration rates follow that trend, by 1990 many states might find themselves with relatively new correctional facilities that are as superfluous as the under-utilized elementary schools in many cities.

The nonprison alternatives

The choices facing the states are all unappealing. Those that are jamming too many prisoners into too little space can continue on the same course, risking at any time a Santa Fe or a court order requiring them to release inmates or build new prisons. Alternatively, the states can start on the expensive avenue of building new facilities now, without the prodding of a court order. But there is another option, as well: State legislators, prosecutors and judges could reexamine the sentencing policies that are behind the influx of inmates into a system that cannot handle them.

Now that few criminal-justice experts put much stock in the ability of prison programs to rehabilitate inmates, the rationale behind those long sentences is a mixture, in most cases, of deterrence, retribution (or "commensurate deserts" as it is also called) and incapacitation of the offender. The latter is an increasingly common justification for long sentences.

But just how much crime can a sentencing policy of "getting them off the streets" actually head off?

This statistical question is worth asking because the policy of using long sentences to incapacitate the most active criminals is

based on the very practical claim that it at least can have a substantial effect on the crime rate. Like many claims and hypotheses
in the criminal-justice field, this one is difficult to prove or disprove
definitively, but there are at least some indications that society will
get relatively little return from long sentences—unless it intends to
use them on a scale that will bust budgets from one coast to
another.

Incapacitation would work better if it were not for the fact that
most offenders do not go to prison until they are in their early or
mid-twenties. By this time, most have their really high-crime years
behind them. Eighteen-year-olds, after all, were arrested for committing more robberies in 1981 than persons of any other single
age. There are excellent reasons for the delay between an offender's
highest crime years and an actual prison sentence. It usually takes
that long for the criminal-justice system to recognize that a given
offender is becoming a career criminal. A crystal-ball profile that
made use of information about an offender's employment and
drug history and could tell judges which first- or second-offender
was on his way to making a life of crime would reduce this delay,
but some of the shortcomings of predictive profiles were spelled
out in the chapter before this one.

In 1978, the National Academy of Sciences did a "cost-benefit"
analysis of incapacitation. Its conclusion was that in order to
achieve a 10 percent reduction in crime by this method, California
would have to increase its prison population by 157 percent, New
York by 263 percent and Massachusetts by 310 percent. This
would increase New York's inmate population to almost 100,000,
or about one-fourth of the current *national* total. "The severity and
scale of this punishment and the amount of money we would have
to pay in order to inflict it are almost unthinkable," *Overcrowded
Time* observes.

In his first of two *Working Papers* articles in 1982, sociologist
Elliott Currie hypothesizes tripling the nation's inmate population
to achieve a reduction in crime, through incapacitation, of 20
percent. This would, he estimates, cost about $40 billion in new
construction and require an extra $8 billion annually in operating
costs, not to mention the costs of the additional police and court
staff that would be required. "All of this," Currie wrote, "would
assure an incarceration rate ranging up to more than twenty times

the rate prevailing in some western European countries. It would still leave us with the highest rates of serious violent crimes in the developed world."

A projection of this kind is a *reductio ad absurdum* of the incapacitation approach. Long before any state would pursue mandatory sentencing to this extreme, it would run out of money. But this kind of analysis should serve the useful purpose of getting state legislators and criminal-justice officials to think more seriously than they have about some of the alternatives to long sentences as punishment for felony offenders.

A call for more innovative approaches in sentencing was made in March of 1983 by Attorney General William French Smith. In the first major address of his term on the subject of prisons, Smith said: "We must recognize that we cannot continue to rely exclusively on incarceration and dismiss other forms of punishment." He said that his Justice Department would search for ways to punish nonviolent offenders short of sending them to prison. While prison, he said, makes sense for "murderers, rapists, other violent criminals, drug traffickers and habitual offenders," in other cases the cost of incarceration to society is "too high a price."

Smith's speech is interesting both because of the promise it offers of new Justice Department initiatives in this area and also because it indicates that a national consensus may be forming on the need to broaden sentencing alternatives. By some measures, his suggestion that "nonviolent offenders" be punished with non-prison sentences could reduce the U.S. prison population by almost one half. The phrase "by some measures" is used advisedly, because the distinction between a violent and nonviolent offender cannot always be made neatly. Burglars are generally classified as nonviolent, even though their criminal activity carries with it a high risk of violence if it is disrupted by the person whose home or shop is being burglarized. In some states that have traditionally had low incarceration rates, Smith's suggestion is already being followed on a de-facto basis. His proposal will have the most potential for reducing prison and jail populations in those states, including several in the South and Southwest, that have been willing to use incarceration as a punishment for much less serious crimes.

Probation versus prison

Statistically, nonprison sentences are, even at this time of high incarceration rates, far more common than prison sentences. Of the nearly two million Americans who, in 1981, were under some form of correctional supervision, 63 percent were on probation. About half of them had been convicted of felonies, the other half of misdemeanors. An additional 11 percent of the two million are on parole, i.e., supervised conditional release after serving a portion of a prison sentence; 18 percent are in prison; and 8 percent are in jail. The obvious source of concern for those experts in the field who are worried about the overcrowding of prisons is that prison populations rose by 12.1 percent in 1981 and the number of probationers by just 9 percent. The number of persons on parole went up by less than 2 percent, a rather startling indication of the degree to which states are, for good or ill, giving up on this traditional safety valve of the corrections system.

Some of the support for probationary sentences comes from those same studies that demonstrated that no rehabilitation program is much more effective than any other at reforming the recidivist one-third or one-quarter of all convicted felons. While those studies struck supporters of tough sentencing as a good reason to base punishment strictly on nonrehabilitative goals, such as incapacitation, one could argue just as cogently that if the reconviction rate cannot be affected appreciably by a stint in prison versus a stint on probation, there is a strong argument for reserving the prison sentence for the most serious offenders whose continued freedom society simply will not tolerate.

One state that is making special efforts to develop community-based alternatives to prison is Minnesota. In 1973, Minnesota passed a Community Corrections Act under which the state distributes funds to communities that take the initiative of developing their own corrections programs. These can include intensive probation, weekend detention, community service and treatment for alcohol or drug problems. One secret of the Minnesota law's success, according to *Overcrowded Time*, is its localized approach. This, the publication states, "encourages grassroots participation in the system, which makes the idea of nonprison punishment more understandable to citizens." It also reportedly makes judges more willing to use the alternatives. At least three other states, including Ohio, Oregon and Kansas, have tried the Minnesota approach.

Two of the sentencing alternatives that Attorney General Smith specifically suggested are community service and restitution programs for victims. Both of them have been developed to a high degree in the Quincy, Massachusetts, court of Judge Albert Kramer. In the eight years that his repayment program has been in effect, collections have risen from $38,000 a year to more than a quarter-million dollars. That, according to Judge Kramer, exceeds all the money collected in all of the probation departments of the city of New York.

Offenders in Judge Kramer's court have, as a rule, three choices. If they would rather not pay for their crime by doing time for it, they can do free community work or work to pay restitution to the victim. "If they succeed in that," Judge Kramer said in an ABC interview, "and pay the victim and pay their just debt and make reparations, then we're prepared to release them from going to jail in nonserious offenses. In serious offenses, we perhaps reduce the sentence somewhat for that act."

Judge Kramer believes that this kind of contract involving the court, the offender and the victim often assuages the victim's desire for retribution better than a jail term. "What [victims] are not satisfied with," the judge said, "is having somebody released from jail without [the victims'] participation, or released from their responsibility of paying their debt without paying back the victim or doing something for the community." While Judge Kramer does not advocate his kinds of alternative sentences in cases of murder, he thinks they can be used as punishment in some forms of violent crime. He said, for instance, that if excessive drinking was a cause of the violence, an offender might be required to go to five Alcoholics Anonymous meetings a week and might be subjected to an evening curfew. If the offender misses a meeting, the judge said, he can face a week or two in jail.

In any case, the judge pointed out, murder is a rare crime. With the kinds of sentences his court dispenses, on the other hand, ". . . we can deal with an awful lot of people who are now in our prison systems that can be productive working in a community, paying a victim—and for whom we're not paying a second price for keeping them in prison or jail."

Putting parole on trial

Any description of the criminal-justice system is a description of the use of discretionary power, from the policeman on the beat ignoring a marijuana smoker to the parole board cutting short the sentence of a convicted felon. Of all of these exercises of discretion, one of the most controversial is parole. Although it became after its introduction in New York state in the 1880s so well-accepted a correction practice that every state eventually adopted it in one form or another, it is under sharp criticism a century later.

The chief argument against it is that parole boards have no clairvoyant powers and cannot offer any guarantees that the prisoner they release before the full term of his sentence will not commit a further crime. Beyond that, say the critics, prisoners' parole hearings are often cursory affairs, with little or no input from victims or law-enforcement officials in the prisoner's hometown, and once inmates are on parole, the limited supervision of parolees provided by parole officers offers society little protection against a released prisoner who is determined to get into trouble once again. Even inmates have arguments with parole: The decisions made by parole authorities are often capricious; parole encourages inmates to enroll in rehabilitation programs for insincere reasons; and it forces inmates to live in an atmosphere of stressful uncertainty.

Most defenders of parole will concede that each of these arguments has a degree of merit and that, like all elements of the criminal-justice system, parole would function better if it were more amply funded. But their counter to criticism is a question of their own: Will mandatory, nonparolable sentences or other alternatives to parole work any better?

By some measures, parole works quite well. In 1980, 25 percent of parolees were returned to prison, most of them for violations of parole conditions and not for outright crimes. Nationally, according to Edward Hammock, former chairman of the New York State Parole Board, the rate of recommitments for criminal violations was less than 10 percent. In his own state, says Hammock, where more than 60 percent of inmates are turned down for parole at their first hearing after becoming eligible, the rate of recommitments for committing an actual crime lately has been less than 5 percent. This is not, as was pointed out earlier, a definitive measure of backsliding by ex-convicts. Clearly there are some parolees who commit crimes without coming to the attention of their parole officers or the police. Still, said Hammock in an interview with ABC News, "most of the poeple who go to prison anywhere in this country don't go back. And if that's the fault of the system or happens in spite of the system, then it certainly is good." If all former prisoners *did* revert to criminal activities after their release, the United States would have no civil peace at all. There are, Hammock said (citing a *New York Times* statistic), fifteen million former state and federal prisoners walking the streets of this country.

One argument that parole defenders make against those who would replace it with mandatory or strictly determinate sentences is that parole at least gives officials another chance to consider an offender's development before requiring him to complete what may be an unnecessarily long sentence or releasing him. Without a parole system, an inmate who has served his allotted sentence of two, three or five years but is still demonstrably unsuited for life in the community will be released willy-nilly, with no supervision. "What I suggest," said Judge Burton Roberts of the New York State Supreme Court in an ABC-News interview, "is that when a person is released on parole and is monitored and given job habits and has a sword of Damocles over his head that he'll be returned to prison if he doesn't watch his step, that provides a greater deterrent than just keeping him locked up. You can't keep him locked up forever. They don't put people in jail forever for a pocketbook swipe."

To argue against parole of any form, defenders of the system say, one has to have extraordinary faith in the sentencing practices of judges or, in the case of statute-mandated sentences, state legislators. "The judge sitting in court," Hammock said, "when he imposes a sentence on January 1, 1980, is in no position to decide on what's going on with the offender sentenced in 1980 when he comes up to see the parole board in 1986. So somebody ought to find out what's different about this guy in 1986 from what we saw in 1980. That's a function of the parole board." Hard-core critics of parole might concede that significant changes could occur during a prisoner's term, but, many would argue, sentence length should be based strictly on the seriousness of the crime and the criminal's record of past offenses, not on any real or perceived rehabilitation in the offender.

"The heat comes to us"

The public focuses not so much on the theory-of-punishment issues that underlie the parole debate as on the occasional parolee who commits a crime. Indignation over such cases is obviously a factor when, as has happened recently, state legislatures abolish or strictly limit parole. Parole officials concede that their system is not infallible and contend that no other would be, either. "You know, a parole officer has no magic, just like the [parole] board doesn't," said Hammock. "And if a man decides that he wants to offend again, there's not a heck of a lot the P.O [parole officer] can do except try to be a bulwark against that. The heat comes to us because we had him last."

The "heat" that Hammock refers to is being felt not just by parole boards but by everyone in the criminal-justice system. Prosecutors are losing the enormous degree of discretion that plea-bargaining has given them, and judges are having their hands tied by new sentencing laws. "We're a country that always thinks in extremes, particularly about criminal justice," said Alan Dershowitz, a professor of law at Harvard, in an ABC-News interview. "Either we have to have total discretion or we have to have no discretion. The pendulum swings in very wide arcs. A more sensible approach would be to limit discretion ..."

One possibility is that as the public is made more aware of the cost to the corrections system of incarcerating so many offenders, it will inevitably reconsider the course on which the criminal-justice system has been set. At some point, taxpayers will recoil at seeing so much of their money going to buy new prison cells, each of which costs as much as a single-family house, or to maintain an offender in prison at an annual expense that matches the cost of a year at the Harvard Medical School.

Donald J. Newman, the dean of the School of Criminal Justice at the State University of New York in Albany, made an eloquent plea for maintaining the parole system in an article in the *New*

York Times in 1981. He sounded a hopeful note with regard to parole that could be extended to nonprison sentence alternatives as well: "In the long run, the political system responds to cost effectiveness." In this case, if the political system doesn't, the results are all too foreseeable: explosions in prison costs, explosions in prison frustrations.

Chapter 9

"An anxious concern for victims"

There is no victim-justice system. We're trying to get the victims some kind of emotional restitution by counseling. We're trying to get them some sense of capacity to deal with their own lives again, that someone cares. And this is not something that happens in the criminal-justice system. The criminal-justice system is set up to punish criminals; victims are nonpersons in the criminal-justice system.

—Joan Garland of Scarsdale, New York,
mother of a homicide victim and co-founder,
with her husband, of a nonprofit
organization to help victims of violent
crime in their area.

ne point above all became clear in ABC News' examination of crime in this country: There is very little consensus on most of the crucial controversies in the criminal-justice system. Reasonable men and women argue quite reasonably for and against plea-bargaining, mandatory sentences, parole and the proper functions of the juvenile courts. On one issue, however, there is very little disagreement—that the system has not given sufficient attention to the needs of the victim, and something should be done about this.

Not everybody comes to this conclusion from the same direction. Conservatives tend to say, "The system has extended too many rights to criminals, it's only fair that victims have some." A political expression of this point of view is the Proposition 8 that California voters passed in June 1982. Called "the victims' bill of rights," Proposition 8 helped victims by establishing restitution procedures and giving them a formal role in sentencing and parole hearings. It also cut into defendants' rights by making it more difficult for them to secure pretrial release and by stripping some of the protection defendants have had against illegally seized evidence.

Liberals also support greater concern for victims, but on the grounds that society has an obligation to ensure that no one suffers unduly from a social problem. There is also concern, shared by conservatives, that the criminal-justice bureaucracy should be as responsive as possible to the mostly poor individuals who become involved in it as victims or witnesses. "The most discriminated-against person in the whole system is the inner-city victim," Norval Morris of the University of Chicago said in an ABC-News interview. But, he said, many of those who complain about the system not taking victims seriously then go on to call for more severe punishments for the criminals, "which isn't the point at all. It's an independent question. The immediate question is, what about treating the victims with respect, taking an interest in their cases, helping them in the court, and if necessary see that they don't lose financially by their loss."

The growing casualty list

If there is such broad political agreement that society has done badly by crime victims, why did this not become a subject of widespread attention until the late 1960s and 1970s?

A partial explanation is that it took the increasing crime rates of those years to bring home to society just how pervasive the crime problem was becoming. Each year, even when the crime rate declines slightly, crime is taking new casualties. The emphasis on the sheer numbers of crime victims in the United States became institutionalized in the early 1970s with the National Crime Survey, a collection of victimization statistics that showed that the public was suffering at least twice as many crimes as were being reported to police. These discrepancies between the crime-incidence figures of the victimization survey and the data of the FBI's Uniform

Crime Reports put in sharp relief how little faith victims have in the system's capacity to redress the wrongs done them.

Further evidence of the impaired relations between victims and the system came when researchers sought to find out why approximately 50 percent of all cases in which an arrest had been made were dropped from the criminal-justice system. A major reason for this, it turned out, was lack of victim or witness cooperation. In many instances, this was due to a change of heart on the part of a victim who had a prior relationship with the defendant. But in other cases, victims stopped cooperating with police and prosecutors because they were treated insensitively or forced to make numerous reappearances in court as cases were continued. As police and prosecutors were made more aware of this explanation for the collapse of cases, they became more interested in tending to the needs of victims and witnesses.

According to one analysis of the victims' movement, it owes its origin in part to the many rape crisis centers that were established around the country in the late 1960s and 1970s. These centers were a response to a specific shortcoming of the criminal-justice system: its failure to deal sensitively with the emotional needs of the victims of this highly traumatic crime. Before long, John Blackmore wrote in a 1979 article on the victims' movement in *Police* magazine, police departments were setting up their own sexual-abuse units, staffed primarily by woman officers who were trained in crisis intervention and counseling. Blackmore believes that this initial concern over rape victims eventually "spearheaded" the broader attempt to improve the status of all of the "nonpersons" of the criminal-justice system, as Joan Garland refers to victims.

One additional factor in society's newfound concern for victims was the perception that crime victimization was part of the malaise of the inner-city ghetto. As society became more conscious of the ghetto in the 1960s as a social problem, it focused more on the fact that inner-city blacks suffer disproportionately as victims of crime. According to the ABC crime poll, four out of ten people living in all-black neighborhoods have at least once been the victim of criminal violence; seven in ten have suffered property crime. One in ten residents of all-white neighborhoods has been a victim of violent crime; four in ten have been victims of property crime. As politicians have become more aware of ghetto residents' intense concern over crime, all politicians, liberals or conservatives, have found it easy to address the crime problem by making politically unassailable statements about society's need to do more for crime's victims.

More rhetoric than money for victims

The proof of politicians' sincerity on this issue can be found in the resources they are willing to devote to it. The record is mixed. Many of the first victim-assistance programs were set up with grants from the now-defunct federal Law Enforcement Assistance Administration. LEAA sent more than $80 million to state and local government units for victim- and witness-assistance programs. But when the grants expired, so did seven of the ten programs studied by Alan T. Harland of the Criminal Justice Research Center in Albany, New York, who did a report on the victim-assistance movement for the Justice Department in 1981. "It's a popular, hot political issue, like apple pie and motherhood. But when it comes to money, it's not there," he said in a 1981 interview with the *Christian Science Monitor*.

In 1982, Congress passed legislation that did several things for victims: It imposed penalties on persons who try to intimidate witnesses or victims; it required sentencing reports in federal-court criminal cases to include statements concerning the impact of the crime on the victim; and it both authorized judges to order restitution to a victim and required judges who do not order restitution in a given case to explain that decision. But the period of federal subsidies for victim programs is past. Washington plainly expects the programs to have established enough local support to keep them going on their own steam. Some will survive this test, some won't. In 1982, Lucy Friedman, the head of New York City's program, told *Editorial Research Reports*: "Victim assistance is a so-called popular movement at the moment. I don't know how long it will stay that way. What's more important is that it stay that way long enough for us to send down our roots."

The primary need of the victim is crisis-intervention counseling, "psychological first aid," in the phrase of Emilio Viano, author of *Victims and Society*. "If a victim gets the right kind of help, right away, it provides a framework for recovery. The next day is not good enough." Therapists who work with crime victims say they typically go through stages. The first is characterized by shock and panic and the second by an emotionally turbulent struggle to come to terms with the violation of the self. The feelings of fear, anger and depression usually subside during the third stage, when the victim's equilibrium is restored. But Blackmore, in his *Police* magazine article, refers to the finding of Dr. Martin Symonds of New York's Karen Horney Institute that many victims suffer a second injury at the hands of insensitive police officers, family members or medical personnel. This second injury, Dr. Symonds says, can cause depression at a point when the person should be recovering from the trauma of the crime. "We have to take care with the victim," Blackmore quotes Dr. Symonds as saying. "Our job is one of restoration and nurturance. We have to give back to the victim the sense of effectiveness and power that the criminal took away."

The victim and the system

Once a victim is past the initial crisis of the crime, he finds himself more and more entangled in the criminal-justice system—assuming he decides to report the crime and cooperate with law-enforcement officials at all. The experience can be a disheartening one, or it can be a satisfying exercise in helping the police to bring the perpetrator to justice. It is never easy, however. Norval Morris pointed out, for instance, that one of the most disconcerting experiences that rape victims have to endure after steeling themselves to pursue charges in the first place is the grand-jury appearance. It is not a public event. The grand jury meets behind closed doors to decide whether the evidence in a case warrants an indictment. But it can be unbearable for a victim to go through an account of the crime while the twenty-three grand jurors, who have just listened to nine or ten similar crime descriptions, talk with one another and pay little heed. "Here you've got sort of a high point for her," Morris said in an ABC-News interview, "and your overloaded, routinized system [responds in that way]. Now, I don't have cheap, quick cures for that, but I see it as a very real problem."

The best victim-assistance programs try to bring victims through experiences like this, but those agencies are more the exception than the rule. According to a 1982 survey of such programs by *Editorial Research Reports*, one of the largest in the country is New York City's Victims' Services Agency. Drawing on federal, state, city and private foundation money, it employs more than 200 and has more than 100 volunteers. Among VSA's various services are an around-the-clock hotline that provides crisis counseling and information on police and court procedures. VSA operates seven community centers around the city to help crime victims in their own neighborhoods; it employs trained locksmiths to repair and change locks at no cost to elderly victims; and it operates special reception centers in borough courthouses for victims and witnesses where they can wait in security (no small matter in urban courthouses) until their cases are called. VSA workers also advise victims and witnesses on the ins and outs of the criminal-justice system and notify them when they are needed to testify in court. The notification procedure keeps citizens from coming to court when their hearings have been postponed or canceled; it also helps to assure that the witnesses or victims *do* appear when the court needs them.

In many jurisdictions, such special programs are probably unnecessary. Police and prosecutors have the time to work with victims and witnesses and treat them as individuals with very specific needs and not just as props in a court case. In other jurisdictions, there is a definite call for agencies like New York's. Paul Garland, co-founder with his wife, Joan Garland, of Crime Victims Assistance Agency, emphasizes how crime victims often feel themselves at sea when they suddenly find themselves thrust by a criminal act into the law-enforcement system: "You have essentially no one to turn to, no one to get advice from, no lawyer available to help you, no source of information that can explain to you what you do next," he said in an ABC-News interview. Comparing this lack of assistance for the victim with the right to counsel and to medical assistance of the defendant, Garland says: "We have a total imbalance at the very beginning of the whole process."

One grievance that victims have often had is over their exclusion from the plea negotiations that take the place of a formal trial in 90 percent of all criminal-court cases. Many jurisdictions that do not have formal victim-assistance programs are trying to meet this criticism by including victims in pretrial conferences or, failing this, by keeping victims well informed of the course of plea negotiations and the basis of the prosecutor's decisions in the negotiation process. Morris, in *The Future of Imprisonment*, makes a particularly strong argument for inviting (but not requiring) victims to attend pretrial conferences in the company of the prosecutor, defense counsel and defendant. He sees in the victim's participation in this process psychological benefits for both the defendant and the victim. Each is helped to see the other as an individual and the victim's consent (if it is given) in the plea negotiation can speed in the offender the process of self-forgiveness that, Morris says, "self-reform presupposes." "A pretrial conference in which the victim agrees does give the convicted criminal, in prison or not, an opportunity to begin again if he wants to—and immediately," Morris writes.

Compensation and restitution

Victim-assistance programs as developed as New York's VSA are still relatively rare, but thirty-seven states and the District of Columbia do have laws on the books calling for financial compensation of victims. Such laws were first enacted as recently as the 1960s, but they have a long and honorable pedigree in ancient law. Compensation was a part of the Babylonian code of Hammurabi, Mosaic law and the penal systems of Athens and Rome. According to *Editorial Research Reports'* survey of the subject, the principle was carried to the furthest degree in Anglo-Saxon England "when set amounts of compensation were established for various crimes." After the Middle Ages, compensation played a lesser role in criminal codes. English reformer Jeremy Bentham did try to revive compensation in the nineteenth century, but by this century both the principle of compensating the victim and requiring restitution from the criminal had been replaced by a system of criminal punishment that incarcerated the criminal and let the victim fend largely for himself.

The thirty-seven programs differ in size, but most are similar in their details. The state will compensate victims for medical or funeral expenses, forgone wages or other financial losses. Most programs offer assistance only if victims are not covered by insurance or government-aid programs; most have maximum grants, of which the highest in 1982 was $50,000. The states require that victims report the crimes within a certain period of time and that they work with the authorities in trying to identify and capture the criminal. Compensation is generally withheld from victims who provoked their crimes or were involved in criminal activities themselves when the incident occurred. In another attempt to keep the programs from being abused, many forbid grants to victims who were related to the criminal or were living with him or her.

According to *Editorial Research Reports*, about half of the state programs are funded directly from general revenues. The rest rely on penalties assessed against offenders or on a mixture of penalties and general revenues. States that have passed compensation laws recently have tended to specify that funding must be from fines or penalties and a few states that had originally relied solely on general revenues are now, under the pressure of tight budgets, switching over at least in part to penalty assessments.

Although compensation of victims by the state is relatively new on the American scene, restitution by criminals of victims' financial losses has always been an element of often informal arrangements made either before trials or as part of a judge's disposition. In 1981, Harland did a study for the Justice Department of the potential role of restitution programs in nonviolent crimes of theft and came up with some encouraging results. Among them was his finding that "relatively few victimizations are so costly as to negate the possibility of a restitutive disposition, even bearing in mind the very low income levels of many defendants." There is no question, he concluded, that systematic restitution could in those cases cleared by an arrest and conviction fill an important role, since only a small percentage of theft victims either recover their stolen money or goods or are compensated for them by insurance.

One of the points that Harland makes about restitution is the uncertainty that exists over whether it is or should be aimed more at the rehabilitation of the offender or the satisfaction of the victim. Criminologists have disagreed on this point, and restitution programs have tended to emphasize one or the other. For Harland, the central question is: "Are there conditions under which restitution can be an effective and appropriate tool for dealing with certain criminal offenders *and* provide a meaningful benefit to the victim? Once the issues are addressed in this light it becomes readily apparent that restitution is part of the ageless correctional dilemma of seeking to balance optimally the interests of the individual offender against those of his victim and of society in general."

The victim-assistance movement owes much of its appeal to the fact that done correctly it can indeed help to restore the balance of interests between the offender and society. The 1981 report of the Attorney General's Task Force on Violent Crime emphasizes that more attention to the needs of victims and witnesses will help the criminal-justice system do its job better. "If victims and witnesses cooperate fully with the criminal-justice system," the report states, "it will be much easier to bring to justice and punish those responsible for breaking the law. Our society will thus become much safer." But beyond that the victim-assistance movement also challenges society to engage in a more energetic effort to reduce crime overall. It is worth noting that victim-assistance programs in some cities have gone beyond that first mission to become informal mediation teams in, for instance, the domestic disputes that underlie so much criminal violence. It should go without saying that a victim-oriented approach to criminal justice is one that is fully committed to reducing victimization by changing the conditions, both inside the criminal-justice system and in society generally, that foster crime.

In the broadest sense, then, the victim-assistance movement carries within it the seeds of policymaking that can redound to the benefit of both victims and defendants. Alan Dershowitz of the Harvard Law School made this point as a member of the same ABC-News panel on victims that Paul and Joan Garland participated in. "I'm very concerned with the rights of defendants," he said, "also very concerned with the rights of victims. For several reasons. Victims and defendants come from the same groups; many defendants have been victims, and most of the effective ways of reducing the number of victims also benefit the defendants. I think what we have to be concerned about is the muscle-flexing of politicians which tries to divide the world into two groups: those who favor the criminals and those who favor the victims. That is a false dichotomy, and I think the work the Garlands are doing is very important in helping us to understand that there are similarities between victims and criminals. There are responsibilities, to be sure, and criminals have to take the responsibility and have to take the punishment for the crimes that they commit."

The issue of victim assistance is distorted by those who say that society has been inordinately solicitous of criminals and now it's the turn of the victims. The neglect of victims has been an indication of the public's preference not to be confronted with the problem of crime at all. The victim-assistance movement, to its credit, is helping to force the issue. For that reason alone, victim assistance—even though it is a newcomer on the criminal-justice scene—deserves a high priority in the distribution of society's limited resources for coping with crime and its effects. In Morris's view, how a law-enforcement system treats victims is one of the best gauges of its quality: "I don't think whether you have put police in one-car or two-car patrols, or whether you have exclusionary rules or don't, and certainly whether you have capital punishment or don't, you're going to make a damn of difference. They keep using the wrong measures of success here. The success should be efficiency, decency, proper balance between state authority and individual freedom, an anxious concern for victims."

Chapter 10

As if it were our child

In large measure, America's crime problem is its youth problem, and vice versa.
—*Franklin E. Zimring, University of Chicago criminologist.*

all it the crime problem or the youth problem, but there is no question that the eleven years between the ages of fourteen and twenty-five are a perilous period for millions of young people. Each year, police arrest for Index offenses about three-quarters of a million youths whose path through adolescence and into adulthood includes a detour into lawbreaking. In 1981, persons seventeen or under accounted for 33.5 percent of all arrests for Index crimes. Young people under twenty made up more than half of all Index-offense arrests—51.5 percent. Their share of property-crime arrests was particularly high—55.6 percent. In 1981, a youngster between the ages of fourteen and seventeen stood about a one in thirty-three chance of being arrested. For all ages, the chance was about one in 100. The public is so wary of teenagers, especially in groups, that in the ABC-News crime poll almost half of those questioned said they would go out of their way to avoid teenagers hanging out on a street corner.

With the falloff in the birth rate over the past fifteen to twenty years, the population of this crime-prone age group has declined and, not surprisingly, the number of young arrested persons has shown the same trend. Between 1977 and 1981, the total number of youths seventeen or under who were arrested for Index crimes fell from 807,638 to 728,815, a drop of 9.8 percent. (Less reassuringly, the number of youths in that age group arrested for violent crimes actually went up over that four-year span by 3.9 percent.) It is difficult to be very encouraged by the victories over crime that the changing population structure provides. All that these victories teach us about offenders is something that we already knew—they are overwhelmingly young. Moreover, the slight and irregular gains that population trends yield could be reversed if and when the birth rate rises again substantially.

Getting an early start

The crime problem is the youth problem, as criminologist Franklin E. Zimring puts it, not just because so many crimes are committed by young people but also because so many adult offenders first come to the attention of the law-enforcement system as juveniles. When Jan M. and Marcia R. Chaiken isolated their "worst 10 percent" of offenders among inmates in several prisons, they discovered that they had typically begun committing crimes before the age of sixteen. They were also more likely than other offenders to have spent time in juvenile correctional institutions. This is by no means proof of the failure of such institutions. It is simply an indication that the worst criminals get an early start in their careers and an early taste of the measures society has at its disposal to punish or rehabilitate them.

The winnowing process that goes on at all stages of the criminal-justice system—the separation of the casual miscreants from the ones who bear the closest watching—is particularly crucial when it comes to juveniles. (For the most part, this chapter will consider juveniles those offenders who have not yet reached the age of eighteen, which is the most common dividing line states have drawn between juvenile and adult courts.) Self-report studies going back to the 1940s have indicated that up to 90 percent of young people commit, at one time or another, an act that could have landed them in juvenile court. Since the purview of juvenile court includes many offenses, such as truancy or running away from home, that are relatively trivial, this should not be so surprising. But these studies and reports that police arrest just one out of five of the juveniles they see violating the law are evidence of how selective everyone in the juvenile-justice system, from police officers to judges, has to be to keep sheer numbers from swamping the system altogether. To a degree, results justify this constant filtering process. Experts in this field point out, after all, that 95 percent of all juvenile delinquents straighten out as they move from adolescence into young adulthood.

One measure of the funneling that occurs in the juvenile system is that while in the adult system about half of all arrests finally end up in court, in the juvenile system the proportion is even smaller. And, while 95 percent of adult cases that are not screened out result in convictions, the percentage of "delinquency" findings (juveniles are not "convicted") in juvenile courts is considerably lower. Less serious offenses involving children who have not been arrested before are typically handled on an informal basis by an intake worker, usually a probation officer, and often after a consultation with the arresting officer.

If a decision is made to refer a case to court, there is first an "adjudicatory" hearing at which the facts of the case are settled, either through the youngster's admission or the presentation of evidence. The judge can then dismiss the case or find the child "delinquent." A "dispositional" hearing follows a finding of delinquency to decide what is to be done with the child.

Juvenile judges as surrogate parents

The nation began treating young arrested persons in this way eighty-four years ago in Chicago, Illinois. From the beginning, the courts were given an extremely broad mission. They would concern themselves not just with young people who had violated criminal statutes but also with those who were in need of supervision because their parents or schools had deemed them uncontrollable. In all instances, the courts' actions would be in the spirit of rehabilitation, not punishment. Because of this, the dispositions arrived at were to reflect not so much the seriousness of the youth's offense as the degree of assistance he or she needed. While this ideal has often been violated by judges whose dispositions are punitive (one report refers to the ideal as a "fairy tale that never came true"), the judges who do pay more than lip service to the philosophy are frequently more willing to confine the child who simply cannot get along with his or her parents than the young lawbreaker. "Nationwide," wrote Charles Silberman in *Criminal Violence, Criminal Justice,* "runaways and incorrigibles (juveniles whose offense is a defiance of parental authority) are more likely than burglars to be incarcerated, and at least as likely to be locked up (often in adult jails) as robbers."

In 1983, juvenile courts are under fire for being both too lenient and too willing to send young people to detention centers or secure treatment facilities. Critics of juvenile-court leniency point to the frequent use, especially in big cities, of probation as the response to youths who are brought in for even their second or third property-crime offense. On the other hand, critics of the courts' severity echo Silberman's concern about the tendency of juvenile-court judges to confine large numbers of young people whose only offense is a breakdown in their relationship with their parents.

These two complaints about juvenile courts are by no means contradictory. They stem quite predictably from that basic juvenile-court philosophy that its interventions are to heal, not to punish. The seriousness of the offense does not determine the disposition; the need of the child does. Unfortunately, a confinement in a secure treatment center may be perceived as a help by a well-meaning judge but as a Dickensian ordeal by the youngster who has to put up with the separation from family and friends and with "treatment" practices that are often crude and unsuited to the child's particular problem.

The guiding principles of juvenile courts are now on trial themselves. Since the 1970s, experts have been recommending fundamental changes in the policies of the courts. One is that dispositions be based less on the perceived rehabilitative needs of the child and more on the seriousness of his offense and his past record. Another is that the juvenile courts relinquish to other social agencies all or virtually all of their jurisdiction over the troubled, "uncontrollable" youngsters who have made up such a large part of their caseloads.

*Keeping life chances
intact*
Both of these issues were addressed
during the late 1970s by a study of the Institute of Judicial Administration of New York University Law School and the American
Bar Association's Commission on Juvenile Justice Standards and
by a report made by the Twentieth Century Fund's Task Force on
Sentencing Policy Toward Young Offenders. On the subject of
making the punishment fit the crime, the task force report, *Confronting Youth Crime*, stated the group's belief that "the degree of
punishment available for youth crime should be proportional to
the seriousness of the offense." The task force acknowledges that
"rehabilitation and helping services are a part of any rational
scheme of dealing with young offenders." But, in place of the
open-ended authority to set dispositions that most juvenile-court
judges now have, the task force recommended that the state legislatures fix maximum periods for confinement or probation of a
juvenile found to have committed a given offense; that judges
make the crucial decision of whether the delinquent goes to an
institution; and that a "centralized correction authority" be empow-
ered to set release dates short of the maximum.

The task force made it quite clear that it did not intend that its
recommendations become an excuse for far more severe juvenile
sentencing practices than now prevail. Emphasizing the need to
give youngsters in trouble a chance to pass through their crime-
prone stage "with their life chance intact," the task force called for
minimizing stigma and confinement. While no young person
should get the impression from the juvenile-justice system that
crimes go unpunished, the report states: "Giving young offenders
a chance to reform is intelligent social policy. Such a policy involves
risks and costs; a considerable minority of young offenders may
not outgrow their propensity to crime. But there is no evidence
that secure confinement is more effective than lesser measures in
dissuading young offenders from pursuing criminal careers."

One of the points made by the task force and other critics of the
juvenile-justice system is that officials make excessive use of
pretrial detention in the juvenile equivalent of jails as a way to
"teach the kid a lesson." Pointing out that ten times as many
juveniles are incarcerated before their trials as after them, the task
force report called punitive pretrial detention "inappropriate and

unjust." In its place, the report recommended community supervision or some form of nonsecure housing as ways to assure that juvenile defendants do not flee before their trial. If detention is necessary, the task force said, there should be both judicial and administrative monitoring of it.

Juvenile courts have traditionally had greater discretion in confining defendants before trial than adult courts have had. State and federal laws permit holding adult defendants without bail or on high bail only insofar as it is necessary to assure their appearance in court for trial. Any danger that the defendant might pose during the period until trial is not supposed to enter into the decision to release or not to release (although it often does in practice). In juvenile courts, on the other hand, laws have permitted detaining an accused youth if a judge determines that there is a serious risk he or she would commit a crime if released.

In April of 1983, the U.S. Supreme Court agreed to hear a New York case that could put an end to this freer use of detention in juvenile systems. A federal District Court and the U.S. Court of Appeals for the Second District have already ruled that the New York law permitting such a distinction between juvenile and adult pretrial detention is unconstitutional. The appeals court, basing its decision on the due-process clause of the Constitution, came to the conclusion that because most of the juveniles who were detained were either found not guilty or were released after trial, pretrial detention was being used "to impose punishment for unadjudicated criminal acts" and not primarily to prevent crimes. The city and state have argued that they should be allowed to take the safety of the community into account at the pretrial stage even if most of the detainees are eventually released by the courts. If the Supreme Court should uphold the lower court rulings, it would mean that juveniles could be held in such facilities only as a way to assure their appearance at trial. While such a decision would not necessarily eliminate the punitive use of detention, it would substantially increase the burden on authorities to justify this form of confinement.

At least as controversial as the question of whether juvenile dispositions should be based on the delinquent's treatment needs or the seriousness of his offense is the contention that juvenile courts should largely end their involvement in noncriminal matters like uncontrollability. When the American Bar Association's

Commission on Juvenile Justice Standards first proposed this at an ABA convention in 1979, it was tabled for a year and then considered gain in 1980. After strenuous objections to the proposal from juvenile-court judges, the House of Delegates in 1980 voted 145-142 not to adopt it.

The position of the Commission on Juvenile Justice Standards was that the 500,000 children who come into the courts not as criminals but as "persons in need of supervision" (or PINS, as many states refer to them) should not be subject to confinement for acts that would not be considered criminal if committed by an adult. Such confinement is especially undesirable, critics of this practice say, when PINS are placed in the same institutions as more hardened young criminals. Instead, the commission said, virtually all PINS children should be placed under the authority of social services or "crisis intervention" networks.

In Zimring's background paper to *Confronting Youth Crime*, he presents a compelling argument for a middle ground on this issue, arguing that it should not be governed by "abstract principles." He favors whatever is the "less harmful alternative" in choosing "between the dangers of overintervention and those of under-intervention." If a state does choose to reduce the jurisdiction of its juvenile courts in noncriminal cases, he cautions, it will have to provide "services for the child at war with the values or custody of his family.

"Persistently disobedient children," he writes, "are among the most difficult cases encountered by the courts, social agencies and institutions that handle them. This is an area where there are no totally right answers."

Adult trials for juvenile offenders?

At the same time that some critics of the juvenile courts are trying to take their noncriminal business from them, other critics contend that the juvenile courts should lose their authority over the most serious criminal cases. In forty-eight of the fifty states, there are already provisions for the transferring or "waiving" of certain juvenile defendants accused of serious felonies to the adult criminal court. As a rule, this procedure is reserved for an extremely small minority of severe cases. In 1977, public dissatisfaction with the juvenile courts in New York State led to passage of a law that required that cases of juveniles aged thirteen to fifteen charged with serious felonies *begin* in criminal court. The law, which went into effect in 1978, also spelled out for different offenses the maximum sentences for young offenders, all of which were less severe than the standard adult sentences but more severe than the limited dispositions allowed in juvenile court.

Not unexpectedly, the reaction of the criminal courts was to "waive" back many of the cases to juvenile court. In 1980, according to the *New York Times*, 63 percent of the juvenile cases entered in adult court were either dismissed or sent to juvenile court. In cases that stayed in the adult court, the *Times* found, the judges rarely imposed the stiff penalties allowed by the law. This result is in line with a study done in other states for the U.S. Justice Department of juvenile cases that are sent up to an adult court. The pattern, according to the research done by the Academy for Contemporary Problems, based in Columbus, Ohio, is that judges in adult courts rarely give juvenile offenders long sentences. As incorrigible as a young offender may seem, judges are understandably reluctant to consign youths to the brutal conditions that often obtain in state prison cellblocks. In fact, one of the strongest arguments against trying any but the most serious juvenile cases in an adult court is that the judge is less likely than a juvenile judge to be familiar with the available range of correctional facilities and programs for young people.

Does more severe sentencing in adult courts deter young delinquents? Frank Hall, who until recently was director of New York's Division for Youth, doubts it. "I think back to when I was young," he said in an ABC-News interview. "You know, most kids don't think beyond lunch. They're not planning ahead; they're not thinking about the consequences of their actions.

"I think people have to be held accountable for their actions," Hall said, "but I don't think that means we lock them up and give up on them and assume that somehow getting them off the streets is going to solve the problem. Ultimately they all come back, sooner or later. At some time, they all come back."

On one issue related to juvenile delinquency, there is less disagreement: that the juvenile records of youthful adult offenders should be available to prosecutors and judges in the adult system.

In some jurisdictions, transfer of such records has been routine; in some it is prohibited by confidentiality rules or laws; and in many, as was mentioned in Chapter 3, the transfers could take place but don't for reasons of sheer bureaucratic inertia. The Twentieth Century task force recommended that adult-court officials be given access to a defendant's juvenile record *after* a judge has found probable cause to believe the defendant guilty of the crime charged. This, they said, would provide sufficient protection that a person's juvenile record would not be gratuitously exposed, but it would also assure that in processing the defendant's case past the probable-cause stage, the system would not treat him with the leniency usually extended to a genuine first-offender.

In the opinion of many experts in the field, regular use of juvenile records in adult courts would be one of the most effective steps the system could take to identify those offenders whose background of repeated or violent crimes would make them candidates for fairly severe sentencing even after a first or second adult offense. In "Identifying Serious Offenders," a report that was presented in 1982 to a Harvard conference on the criminal-justice system, Barbara Boland of INSLAW concluded: ". . . more and more it appears the notion that youthful mistakes should not be allowed to destroy an entire life is giving way to the view that youthful offenders when they reach the adult court should not be allowed to begin with a fresh slate."

Juvenile-court judges' limited options

Much of the public's discontent with juvenile courts should more fairly be directed at the sentencing options—or lack of same—that the courts have at their disposal. Especially in big cities, the availability of good programs willing to take adolescent offenders, particularly ones with a history of violence, is extremely limited. Often, a judge is faced with a choice between sending a youngster to an overcrowded training school or putting him on probation. Unless the probation is done more intensively than is usually the case in large cities, this disposition is often seen as a slap on the wrist by the arresting police officer, any victims of the offense and the delinquent himself. The problem of inadequate sentencing alternatives exists whether young offenders' cases are handled in adult courts or juvenile courts. The Twentieth Century Fund task force states in no uncertain terms that "... no sentencing policy is any better than the facilities we use to deal with the young offender."

The 1960s and 1970s were a period of considerable innovation in this area, with some new initiatives giving indications at least of a measure of progress in helping young people to break criminal habits or at least to commit less serious crimes. Regrettably, little solid research has been done to confirm these hopeful results by measuring the performance of participants against "control" groups. What is often apparent in these programs moreover is that one may be well suited for one type of troubled adolescent but not for another. Studies of rehabilitation programs for delinquents have turned up more than just a couple of instances in which participants ended up committing more crimes than a control group that had been left to its own devices. Whenever a juvenile probation officer or judge weighs sending a youngster to a community-based program or a secure training school, he has to keep in mind that the vast majority of young people grow out of their troublemaking phase on their own, or at least without the ministrations of the courts.

H.L. Mencken reduced the dilemma of would-be helpers to its simplest terms: "When A annoys B or injures B on the pretense of improving B, A is a scoundrel." Juvenile courts must be constantly alert to the fact that an ill-advised disposition can be as harmful to a young person going through a difficult period as the wrong medicine can be to a sick person. "Nothing that we are doing right now demonstrably works," concluded Franklin E. Zimring in a 1982 interview with the *New York Times*. "If anyone has a program for juvenile crime that he says will make a statistical dent in the problem, he is operating on sheer faith. There are no panaceas nor any general theory that bears endorsement."

For the judge sitting in juvenile court, the problem is complicated, as mentioned above, by the fact that so many of the agencies (including public mental-health facilities) that are in theory available to help the adolescent offender are particular about the type of youngsters they will accept. Their reluctance to deal with the most violent offenders is understandable. Directors of good programs fine-tune the treatment they provide to a certain range of antisocial behavior and cannot be expected to change practices radically to accommodate the tiny minority of violent, uncontrollable youths.

In his 1978 book, *Violent Delinquents*, Paul A. Strasburg, who later headed New York City's Department of Juvenile Justice and is now consulting in the field, looked at a wide range of sentencing and treatment alternatives and came to a number of conclusions. One was that "probation alone is largely ineffective as a sanction or as a treatment." With less serious delinquents, Strasburg wrote, probation might be useful if it were handled by an unusually qualified probation officer or combined with other services. But these circumstances are more the exception than the rule, especially in large cities.

At the other extreme, Strasburg concluded that training schools are not much good either, unless they are held to a small size: "In spite of much rhetoric to the contrary, treatment and rehabilitation are largely absent from the training school setting." Not the least of the problems with these institutions, he points out, is that the most serious delinquents are mixed with less serious offenders. For an age group that is as easily swayed by peer pressure as this one, that mixture can be a sure prescription for aggravating the problems of the less serious offender. Strasburg looked at a number of studies that have examined the records of youths placed in secure institutions of one kind or another and found strong evidence in the research that between 50 and 95 percent of the youths do not need such confinement. Deciding which delinquents *do* need this and which don't is no easy matter, but at least one state, Massachusetts, has managed in the past decade to reduce its secure placements for juveniles to a minimal number without bringing on an epidemic of juvenile crime.

Milieu therapy

Between the extremes of probation and training school, Strasburg finds that various "milieu therapy" programs offer more hope for adolescent offenders than less intense programs or one-on-one sessions with psychiatrists or psychotherapists. "In essence," says Strasburg, "milieu therapy seeks to convert every aspect of the child's environment into a reinforcement of treatment." He describes it as "a total attack on antisocial and self-destructive behavior patterns." What these programs and less intensive group therapies have in common, according to Strasburg, is the goal of bringing delinquents to a point where they can "relate to other human beings with trust, respect and concern." To get to this point, the participants in such programs are helped to develop an awareness of their own feelings and how to express them, a "core of self-respect" and an ability to control their impulses. These are capacities that most individuals develop on their way to maturity, Strasburg observes, and "these therapies attempt to provide the setting and ingredients necessary to permit the growth process to begin again."

One milieu-therapy program that does take hard-core delinquents is a camp in Florida that subjects its participants to a routine of hard labor and strict, virtually military discipline. There is extremely close supervision and strict rules against swearing, smoking, gambling and fighting for the fourteen participants. An ABC-News correspondent described the camp scene this way: "Since the kids here are among the most dangerous in Florida and in the nation, the camp is located in the middle of nowhere on the outskirts of the Everglades. It is surrounded by woods and creeks and swamps filled with alligators and snakes, wild hogs and mosquitoes. Escape is almost impossible. To the kids who come from the inner city, this place is like being on another planet—just what the counselors want."

The camp experience is not the end of the program, either. Bob Weaver, vice president of the Associated Marine Institute, said in an ABC-News interview: "Many programs have been successful in wilderness atmospheres such as this in changing kids' behavior. The difference is going to be, we're going to follow them into the community, give them six months of educational and vocational training after they get back to Miami or whatever large city they're from, and then after that educational and vocational training we're going to place them in jobs and follow them up." Strasburg, too, emphasizes the importance of follow-up in making sure that therapy gains do not vanish.

One residential program that uses a more familylike atmosphere in place of the boot-camp regimen of the Everglades camp is the House of Umoja in Philadephia. Started in 1969 by Sister Falakah Fatah, a woman who was upset when her son joined one of the many gangs in the city, the house of Sister Falakah and her husband, David, has become a surrogate home over the years for 500 gang members. At first, many came right off the streets of their own accord. Now, the fifteen residents are referred from courts.

The day at the house begins with an early-morning breakfast with Sister Falakah and ends with evening recreation and then lights out at ten P.M. In between, there are classes conducted at the school and work, either as a guard in a security service run by the house or as a laborer learning construction skills on one of the twenty-three houses the house has acquired and is in the process of renovating. The House of Umoja gets high marks for turning out alumni who have better than average records of avoiding future run-ins with the police. "A lot of the kids that we have," Sister Falakah said in an ABC-News interview, "are not runaways; they're throwaways. For some reason they never really got enough of caring."

The work that the House of Umoja has done with members of Philadelphia gangs parallels efforts all over the country to reduce deliquency by directing gangs away from the inter-gang violence and street crime that plague so many cities with large minority-group populations. Some of the more successful of these programs employ former members of the gang or residents of the gang's neighborhood to steer the youths toward more constructive activities. In other cases, police have tried to concentrate on arresting and convicting gang leaders on the theory that it is the leadership that holds together the groups of youths, many of whom on their own would not commit the crimes that are a result of the peer-group influence of the gang. Sergeant Joe Suarez of the Los Angeles Police Department's gang-control unit told ABC that, in that city, "Our goal is not to eliminate gangs. The gangs have been here for over 100 years and they're gonna be here after we're gone. We're just interested in reducing their activity."

Replacing nonfunctioning families

As a rule, Strasburg does not see much promise in foster-home placement for delinquents, especially the more serious offenders, but he thinks it can be a solution when there is some way to make the relationship more stable than many foster-home situations are. One program that appears to have achieved this, he writes, is Downeyside in Massachusetts. In that program, a carefully selected and trained adult couple agrees to accept a group of as many as six troubled fourteen- to sixteen-year-olds whose original families, in Strasburg's term, are no longer functioning. If both the parents and the youngsters find the situation is working after a trial period of three months, the children are assured that they will stay in their new "family" for three years. In actual practice, many of the Downeyside families maintain their ties even after the formal period of foster care has ended. One of the interesting aspects of the Downeyside approach is that the "parents" take on their new role as a full-time job. After the first year with the youngsters, one of the two is allowed to return to a position outside the home. But the priority that the program insists on for the parents' family role in the home is one of the ways that Downeyside manages with some success to instill in children the feeling that they do belong somewhere and that someone does care for them.

Downeyside does not accept youngsters with severe psychiatric problems nor ones considered too uncontrollable to live in a family situation. Still, it has handled children who were judged to be too violent for other residential programs. For many youngsters, it seems to be an excellent way to provide what Sister Falakah of the House of Umoja was referring to when she said, "There's a nurturing that we all need, somebody who thinks we're great no matter what we've done."

One option that has worked for many disruptive youngsters is enrollment in a special school or special school program (often combined with job experience) that offers fewer frustrations to the student with learning problems than the regular classroom routine does. A strong indication that school frustrations are at the base of much delinquency is the oft-observed fact that many youths' misbehavior goes down markedly as soon as they drop out of school. A good alternative-school program can minimize class-room frustrations *and* help a youth get the basic skills that he or she needs.

Another approach that youth workers say can be effective for the large percentage of youths whose delinquency reflects troubled family relationships is family counseling or therapy. As with so many other responses to delinquency, this one works only under certain conditions.

For youngsters who warrant more supervision than their parents can or will provide, an alternative to a secure facility is the "tracking" system that was developed by Massachusetts' Department of Youth Services and has since been used by other agencies, as well. With this system, a youth worker "tracks" a delinquent from morning wake-up to his school or job, then makes sure that he goes where he is supposed to after that and, finally, shepherds him home for supper and bed. It is not a cheap program. To be effective with the most disobedient youngsters, a tracker has to work on a one-to-one or one-to-two basis, but it is still cheaper than a training school and avoids training schools' unavoidable problem of concentrating too many delinquent youngsters in one facility.

Programs like the House of Umoja, Downeyside and others are heartening evidence that the lack of any demonstrated surefire treatments for juvenile deliquency has not kept many thoughtful and well-meaning people from trying out new and promising approaches. Delinquency takes many forms; coping with it will require a wide range of treatments and punishments, as well as a strong awareness on the part of juvenile-justice professionals that court action for the sake of court action may be more harmful than doing nothing at all. "If rehabilitation has largely failed (and it has)," Charles Silberman wrote in *Criminal Violence, Criminal Justice*, "the remedy is not to abandon the effort with an air of sophisticated disillusionment; it is to try to understand why, and to intensify the search for approaches that offer some hope of working. This, after all, is what we would do if our own children were involved."

Guns on store shelf

Chapter 11

The gun-control crossfire

It is not straight talk to issue resounding statements
on crime control which wholly omit the slightest
mention of guns.

—*Nelson Rockefeller*

o, guns don't kill people, as oppo-
nents of gun control say, but they certainly make it easier for
people to. And while it is difficult to prove that gun-control laws
reduce the incidence of crime, a study done at Northeastern
University in 1979 on the effects of Massachusetts' stiff penalty for
illegal carrying of firearms offers evidence that well-enforced (and
well-publicized) gun-control laws can make it less likely that guns
will be used in crimes that are committed.

Until studies of the Massachusetts law, the best argument in
favor of the effectiveness of gun-control laws in reducing the
severity of crime was the statistical link between states with loose
gun laws and high incidence of gun use in homicides. As the 1967
President's Commission on Law Enforcement and the Administration of Justice states, "Federal Bureau of Investigation statistics
demonstrate that a higher proportion of homicides are committed

with firearms in those states where firearm regulations are lax than in those areas where there are more stringent controls." In 1977, Steven Brill wrote a report on firearm abuse for the Police Foundation in which he established that the link between high gun involvement in crime and weak gun laws extends to other offenses as well.

The one hitch in this part of the case for gun control is that the same cultural factors that make a state prone to gun violence may make it unreceptive to gun-control laws. Thus, the weak laws and the excessive use of guns in crime may not be in a cause-effect relationship; they may both be products of a cultural climate that tolerates easy acquisition of firearms, even if this leads to higher-than-average rates of gun involvement in crime.

The important contribution of studies on the Massachusetts law, which set a one-year mandatory sentence for carrying a firearm without a proper license, is that they indicate that, within a single jurisdiction, a stricter law can have an effect on gun crime. In the two years after introduction of that law, gun homicides in Boston declined by 55.7 percent, according to the Northeastern University study by Glenn L. Pierce and William J. Bowers. Another interesting finding of the Pierce-Bowers study is that the fall-off in gun crimes began before the law's effective date, an indication that the effect of the massive publicity campaign that preceded the effective date may have been as great or greater than the new penalty itself.

Research on the Massachusetts law gives further validity to the conclusion reached by one national crime commission after another that the U.S. crime problem is made more severe and more violent by the lack of controls over the sale and use of firearms. That was the verdict of the 1967 commission, the Milton Eisenhower commission on violent urban crime in 1969 and the Attorney General's Task Force on Violent Crime in 1981.

The wording in those commission reports (and these were not the only ones) tends to be depressingly monotonous. Figures are given on the appallingly high numbers of Americans killed in the most recent year by handguns (50 percent of 20,053 total homicides in 1981) and the total number of handguns in circulation is often listed (more than sixty million in 1983). Mention is usually made of the fact that existing state and especially federal laws are inadequate for effective regulation of guns. The reports often make note of the fact that public-opinion polling invariably shows a substantial majority of the public in favor of reasonable controls. The commissions always recommend tougher laws.

And nothing happens.

*"If Congress meant
what it said . . ."*
The most recent of these reports was the one done in 1981 by the Task Force on Violent Crime of Attorney General William French Smith. Like the others, it stated the obvious: "Crimes committed by individuals using handguns represent a serious problem of violence in our nation" and "federal gun laws have failed in several ways to achieve their intended purpose due to either a lack of adequate enforcement mechanisms or unintended loopholes in existing law." From those sound starting points, the task force went on to recommend an agenda of gun-law reform that included all but one or two of the proposals of Congress's most committed gun-control advocates.

The task force would require individuals to report gun thefts; mandate a waiting period in the puchase of a handgun so that law-enforcement authorities could determine whether the would-be buyer is prohibited under existing federal law from possessing a handgun; close the loophole in the 1968 gun-control law that forbids the importation of "Saturday night special" guns but allows unassembled parts to be shipped in from overseas and put together here; and encourage tougher prosecution and sentencing in criminal cases involving handguns. One of its more intriguing recommendations was for federal research into technical methods for "detecting and apprehending persons unlawfully carrying guns." If this research panned out, it could, as the report says, "provide an important disincentive for the unlawful carrying of such weapons."

Six weeks after the task force report was published, President Ronald Reagan unveiled his crime program. With the exception of an endorsement of tougher sentencing in gun-crime cases, his program omitted each proposal for tightening gun laws that his own attorney general's task force had recommended.

The case for federal action in this area was made forcefully by the then-superintendent of the Chicago Police Department,

Richard Brzeczek, who appeared on "This Week with David Brinkley" on February 13, 1983, with Brinkley, ABC-News correspondent Sam Donaldson and newspaper columnist George Will.

George Will: Superintendent, nothing more amazes and appalls foreigners looking at our country than the prevalence of handguns. It's obviously an issue the political system flinches from coming to grips with, but if you could poll the members of the Chicago Police Department, would they favor strict handgun control?

Richard Brzeczek: I think our agency is unique because we have historically taken a posture or a position for some type of regulation of handguns. We have spoken out—not only myself but my predecessor superintendents have spoken out—concerning the issue of handgun violence or firearm violence not only in our city but nationally. You are right. We are an international disgrace when it comes to firearm violence. But the approach that you're seeing taken, the handgun-registration ordinance in Chicago, the handgun ban in Morton Grove, the registration ordinance in Evansville, Illinois, for example, are nothing more than just local and, in a way, somewhat feeble attempts to deal with the issue because of the commerce in arms itself. The commerce does not look at any boundaries. It transcends local boundaries; it transcends state boundaries. And I think there has to be some type of intelligent response at the federal level.

A few minutes later, Attorney General Smith and FBI Director William Webster joined the program. After the attorney general had discussed some of the anticrime initiatives of the administration, Will again turned the discussion to gun control.

George Will: But Mr. Brzeczek from Chicago just ... asked eight minutes ago—probably not for the first time—for a federal initiative to control handguns. We probably have as many handguns as we have cars in this country. Why is it beyond the wit of man or the courage of the political system at the federal level to restrict the flow of handguns around and into this country?

William French Smith: Well, in terms of, if you're talking about gun control—

George Will: That's what I'm talking about.

William French Smith: —needless to say, that is a debate that's been going on for a long, long time and there are very strong viewpoints on both sides of it.

George Will: But there was a man who is out on the streets with men who are getting shot—the Chicago Police Department—and he says they want more gun control. They can't cope with it at the local level. Can either of you tell me why we don't need a federal handgun control measure stronger than we have?

William Webster: George, we have a statute designed to prevent the flow of so-called Saturday-night specials into this country, which are largely imports. A reading of that act shows that it is not illegal to bring parts into the United States, and factories have been set up to receive legal parts and make legal Saturday-night specials.

George Will: Should that law be changed?

William Webster: If Congress really meant what it said the first time around, it wouldn't take long to correct that situation.

This last answer by Webster touches on the reason behind the skittishness of executive-department officials on this issue. Even those officials who might be eager to oblige all the Superintendent Brzeczeks in this country and tighten enforcement of the federal gun laws (or even introduce new ones) know that they stand little chance of getting a majority in Congress to back them up.

If Congress won't act...

In 1978, the Carter administration decided not to risk a direct clash with Congress by sending to Capitol Hill a formal legislative proposal on gun control. Instead, it chose to make some internal changes in the procedures used by the Treasury Department's Bureau of Alcohol, Tobacco and Firearms to administer existing federal gun laws. Manufacturers and importers would be required to make quarterly reports of all sales to wholesalers and retailers, along with records of any firearms thefts or losses, and the serial numbers of guns would be assigned in a more systematic way than had been the case. The latter step, in particular, was designed to help law-enforcement officials in the tracing of weapons involved in crimes.

As mild as these measures were and in spite of the support of the nation's police chiefs, they came to nought. First the House Appropriations Committee and then the House of Representatives itself approved a rider to a Treasury appropriations bill specifically forbidding the use of any of the appropriated funds for the implementation of the new rules. Both the committee and the House were dominated by members of the president's own Democratic Party, but party loyalty was a notably weak reed in the face of representatives' fear to be on what the gun lobby considered the wrong side of the issue. The Carter administration took no further steps in this area, and the Reagan administration has been equally inactive, although it is reported to be considering a proposal to shift firearms law enforcement from the Bureau of Alcohol, Tobacco and Firearms to the Secret Service, a proposal that in the past has been supported by some advocates of gun control. Not the least of the advantages of such a move is that it would allow better use to be made of the Secret Service's officers, whose work load peaks during presidential election years and then subsides.

In 1983, Congress has at least three gun-related measures before it, but there is no guarantee that it will act on any of them. Among bills that have been introduced on Capitol Hill is a ban (opposed by the National Rifle Association) on armor-piercing ammunition that can go through policemen's, not to mention presidents', protective vests. Another measure, introduced by Senator James McClure of Idaho and Representative Harold Volkmer of Missouri, would weaken the 1968 federal gun-control law, and a third would tighten it in ways that in many respects echo the recommendations of the Attorney General's Task Force on Violent Crime. This bill, introduced in the Senate by Senator Edward M. Kennedy of Massachusetts and in the House by Representative Peter W. Rodino of New Jersey, would require a twenty-one-day waiting period for handgun purchases; forbid the manufacture and sale of concealable, snub-nosed handguns (the accurate range of such "snubbies" was once described by a newsman as the breadth of a card table); require mandatory sentencing for using a handgun during the commission of a crime; tighten restrictions on gun dealers and manufacturers; require that handgun thefts or losses be reported; and prohibit pawnshops from selling handguns.

Whatever steps Congress does or does not take in this area, there is a growing trend for communities to take matters into their own hands and pass tighter gun-control measures than would ever stand a chance of enactment in Washington. Congressional action has always been in the direction of more registration of weapons and tighter control of the industry generally; citizen movements favor outright bans on handguns, with few exceptions allowed. One of the best examples of the latter, the handgun-ban ordinance of Morton Grove, Illinois, was referred to by Superintendent Brzeczek. This ban has so far withstood not only all court challenges but also an attempt by opponents of the ordinance to throw out the village trustees who first enacted it in 1981. The challengers were soundly defeated in the spring of 1983. This leaves the opponents of gun control with just one avenue for having the law reversed—the U.S. Supreme Court. Gun-control advocates say they would like nothing better than to see the case go to the high court, since they are convinced that the court would, once and for all, rule that nothing in the "right of the people to keep and bear arms" wording of the Second Amendment gives individuals an unlimited right to keep and bear handguns.

If the Morton Grove ban is upheld and similar bans proliferate (the village has already received more than 400 inquiries about it), that could have the effect of making the gun lobby more amenable to gun-registration laws that fall short of actual bans. Or, the Morton Grove phenomenon could simply add fuel to the argument of opponents of gun controls that the ultimate aim of gun-control advocates is to outlaw even licensed possession of handguns. Is there any possible compromise between total bans of the Morton Grove variety and the absolutist position of the National Rifle Association, which in recent years has even been supporting congressional moves to weaken the 1968 law?

Building on the 1968 law

In theory, a compromise should not be impossible to arrive at. Properly enforced, the 1968 law would be a good starting point for a rational gun-control policy. As Brill pointed out in his 1977 Police Foundation report, a federal firearms-control agency with sufficient manpower, computer capability and purposeful direction could make substantial progress toward achieving one of the goals of existing federal gun laws: greater control over the interstate black market in guns. By insisting on more thorough record-keeping of the sort that the Carter administration tried to establish in 1978, the Bureau of Alcohol, Tobacco and Firearms would be able to detect more easily any "leaks" from the lawful system of handgun commerce. Information on gun thefts would help the bureau to crack down on this important source of weapons for criminals. According to bureau trace figures and a study of confiscated weapons done by the New York City police, at least 20 percent (and likely more) of all firearms confiscated by police officers have been stolen, either from individuals or companies involved in firearms commerce.

Beacuse the victims of gun theft frequently do not report their losses (and nothing in current *federal* law requires them to), no one knows precisely how many guns are stolen each year. Extrapolating from figures in New York, where handgun licensees *are* required to report thefts, Brill arrived at a figure of more than 200,000 firearms thefts a year, just from individuals. An extrapolation from a Houston study on burglaries, which showed that a firearm is stolen in that city in one of ten burglaries, indicated that the 200,000 figure was probably conservative. "Although the numbers are not clear," Brill observed, "the volume of thefts suggested above indicates that the number of stolen firearms probably equals the *total* number of firearms involved in all reported violent crimes."

The sheer volume of gun thefts, Brill conceded in his report, limits the effectiveness of any effort to keep guns out of the hands of criminals by reducing illegal gun-trafficking. (Such thefts also naturally call into question the wisdom of the homeowner who considers possession of a firearm a sensible act of self-protection. In the high-burglary areas, where the motive for self-protection is the strongest, the homeowner's gun becomes all too easily part of the criminal's arsenal.) But the theft problem is still no reason for the Bureau of Alcohol, Tobacco and Firearms not to make every effort to track down the black-market channels that are responsible, for instance, for the fact that 96 percent of the handguns seized by New York City police and studied in a 1973 bureau research project had been purchased outside of New York state.

"The illegal sale of firearms in many cities may be the most widespread serious federal crime now being committed," Brill wrote. "It is certainly a federal crime that has the most serious impact on the level of violent street crime in the nation's cities. Yet Congress and the executive branch have never given ATF the resources—nor the supervision—that in any way suggest an appreciation of the nature of this law-enforcement problem."

Brill repeatedly drew a parallel with the federal government's far more aggressive enforcement of laws concerning narcotics. If Washington put into gun-law enforcement the resources it assigns to interdiction of the drug trade, the availability of illegal firearms in jurisdictions that have strict local gun laws would be sharply reduced. In Chapter 3, the difficulties of controlling narcotics trafficking were discussed, but Brill argued in his Police Foundation report that contraband guns could be tracked down with greater success. After all, there is a paper trail: All firearms leave the factory with serial numbers, and dealers are required to keep a record of each firearm's first retail sale. Also, guns are much bulkier and more difficult to hide than drugs. A final point that Brill made is that the black-market sellers of guns do not deal with a regular clientele, the way many drug vendors deal with addicts, and would thus be more likely to sell a gun to a first-time customer who is actually an undercover law-enforcement agent. A side benefit of a successful campaign is that by showing the feasibility of throttling the flow across state lines of black-market guns, legislators in states that still have weak laws could be persuaded to put tough statutes on the books.

In March of 1981, immediately after the attempted assassination of President Reagan with a handgun purchased for less than $50 in Dallas, Texas, ABC News discussed gun control with Los Angeles Police Chief Darrell Gates and New York City Police Commissioner Robert McGuire. After Gates questioned the effectiveness of gun laws, McGuire responded that if effectiveness were the only criterion, there would be no laws against narcotics. "Nobody's suggesting we repeal the narcotics laws," he said. "We've got speeders going through traffic signs. We're not repealing our traffic laws. [Gun-control legislation] is one arrow in law-enforcement's quiver, and I think it's a major arrow, to try to get guns off the street, to say no more, to say that we are not a violent society and to start making it a hard message."

*Lack of controls
helps criminals*

Supporters of gun control believe
aggressive enforcement of the 1968 law, combined with congressional enactment of the best features (such as a mandatory waiting
period before purchase of a handgun) of the Attorney General's
Task Force on Violent Crime and the Kennedy-Rodino bill, would
take this country a long way toward a sane stance on handguns. If
the NRA and other gun-owner organizations remain united in
opposition to any of these measures, it is unlikely that Congress
will act. There are signs, however, of disagreement within the gun
lobby over whether an adamant antiregulation posture is still
tenable. What the lobby has to fear is that at some point the
advocates of gun control may well succeed in their efforts to
persuade the public that the unyielding position of the gun lobby
plays directly into the hands of violent criminals.

"Now the most powerful lobby in the United States, as you
know, is the National Rifle Association lobby," Commissioner
McGuire said during the March 1981 broadcast. "And they point
out that registration might mean confiscation. We can't even get
registration through in this country. The Treasury Department
does not have computerized central records of the shipment and
transportation of guns in this country. We can't trace stolen guns
in this country with any ease because of the opposition of the
lobby."

Even with adequate to more stringent gun-control laws and
effective enforcement of them, the United States would probably
still have the most serious problem of gun-related violence in the
industrialized world. But Massachusetts' experience with its law
on illegal carrying of a firearm is encouraging evidence that firearms
statutes can achieve a deterrent goal. Just as guns don't kill people,
gun-control laws won't end crime. But they may well make it less
lethal. Gun-control advocates believe that no other change in the
law-enforcement system would have as immediate an effect on the
severity of the crime problem in this country.

Family Mourning

Chapter 12

Solutions outside the system

For every problem, there is a solution, which is
simple, neat—and wrong.

—*H.L. Mencken*

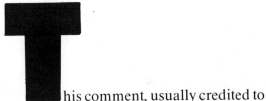his comment, usually credited to
Mencken, on the danger of simplistic solutions should be recited
by state legislators on any occasion when they propose to solve the
crime problem of this country by passing new laws that change the
criminal-justice system. That system is far from perfect—nothing
that is so dependent on the actions and decisions of human beings
could be perfect. But the system could also function much less well
(or more poorly, depending on one's point of view) than it does
now if demands are put on it that are beyond its capacity.

There are signs that this is already happening in the area of
corrections. The warning of likely violence that New Mexico
corrections officials received from an outside observer just before
the Santa Fe prison riot of 1980 should be directed at the country at
large. The nation cannot go on adding each year more than 40,000
inmates to prison facilities of limited capacity without reaping
bloody consequences.

But while there is broad agreement among experts in the field that something has to be done about corrections, there is little faith that investments in this area will have a commensurate effect on the crime rate. The reason that states must either provide more prison space or change their "lock 'em up" sentencing policies is that simple decency requires it. As David Anderson, former editor of Criminal Justice Publications, put it: "If the state assumes total control of a man, body and soul, it reveals much about itself in the way it treats him."

The corrections crisis is an excellent example of something that became apparent during the long months that ABC News explored the crime issue. That issue is complicated by the fact that the public is being sold panaceas that are based on myths and offer little hope of stemming crime. So-called solutions of this kind, such as tampering with defendants' protections against illegal police searches, should be avoided. On the other hand, there *are* measures that should be taken, such as addressing the corrections problem, even though they hold out little short-term prospect of affecting crime.

Another example is in the area of plea-bargaining. Throughout the ABC-News interviews, there were repeated expressions of dissatisfaction with plea-bargaining practices, even among those law-enforcement professionals who defend bargaining as a necessary expedient. Many of the critics, it would appear, would be more willing to accept the practice if it were done in a more formal and regulated way with less of the courthouse-corridor haggling that gives plea negotiations their unsavory reputation. On a short-run basis, procedural change of this kind will probably not affect a jurisdiction's crime problem one iota. In the long run, however, anything that enhances the public's—and especially offenders'—respect for law and the judicial system is a keystone in insuring domestic tranquillity.

A breathing spell for policymakers?

One of the most important potential benefits of the current decline in the crime rate is that it could take some of the pressure off elected officials to come up with quick, often ill-advised solutions, thus encouraging a calmer and more thoughtful response to the crime problem. In a less heated atmosphere, states and cities are more likely to seek solutions to crime in the less visible areas of juvenile-treatment programs and police deployment rather than in drastic changes in the courts, which, as Malcolm Feeley points out, "will always fail" since they are handling society's failures.

Arthur Miller, professor of law at Harvard, posed the question, What would be the best anticrime use of a "bag of money"? His answer was to divide it "probably between the juveniles and the beat police in terms of training, reinforcement and improved police work." He also sees considerable promise in neighborhood watches and citizen patrols.

The best use of police manpower will always depend on the specific characteristics of a city or town, but the research and experience of the past decade indicates, in general, that police procedures that keep officers in the closest possible contact with the public offer the best hope for reducing the fear, and quite often the incidence, of crime. Departments establish this contact in various ways: by creating links with neighborhood block organizations or crime-watch groups, by hiring police auxiliaries from the community, by putting officers on foot patrol or by paying special attention to crime witnesses or victims. There is no single, police-centered answer to fighting crime. As one of the experts ABC interviewed said, if a particular area has a bad burglary problem, the best use of police manpower is in a "sting" operation in which undercover officers make arrests after setting up a phony fencing service for stolen goods.

In the area of juvenile crime, the quick solution is to pass laws requiring that all minors committing serious offenses be tried in adult courts. This solves little, however, if adult-court judges are unaware of good juvenile-treatment programs and are reluctant to send teenaged offenders to adult prisons where their safety cannot be guaranteed. The most urgent need in the juvenile-justice system is for sentencing alternatives, short of training schools, that are effective in protecting society and getting young offenders to change their ways.

As for offenders who have grown out of juvenile courts and have been accused of a crime that has landed them in an adult court, the proposal that court officials have access to their juvenile records is an excellent one. Virtually all courts' sentencing practices take into account a defendant's prior record. Judges making sentencing decisions (and prosecutors negotiating pleas) should know whether a so-called first-offender really is as new to crime as his clean adult record indicates or whether he has several serious juvenile convictions in his past. Again, though, even a sensible (and relatively low-cost) suggestion like this one cannot be counted on to have much effect on crime rates. As long as prisons are as overcrowded and, in many areas, as dangerous as they are, it is doubtful that judges are going to be very severe with a seventeen- or eighteen-year-old convicted of his first adult offense—even if he does have a long juvenile record.

The conclusion that University of Chicago criminologist Franklin E. Zimring came to in an ABC-News interview is worth quoting: "Nobody thinks the criminal-justice system is the principal mechanism that we have for regulating [the] crime rate, or, if they do, they haven't spent much time around contemporary criminal justice in the United States or in other countries."

Getting the public involved

The ABC-News producers and correspondents who did spend some time around the criminal-justice system in the course of preparing their reports would tend to agree with Zimring. This realization of the limits of the system would be more disheartening if it were not for the encouraging fact that the public is finally beginning to recognize that *it* must play a larger role in this area than it has in the past and not rely on undermanned law-enforcement agencies. At one level, this participation takes the form of membership in community organizations, neighborhood-watches or citizen-patrol groups. At another level, citizens are insisting, both through their elected representatives and in referendum votes, that the political system address the crime problem.

So far, the solutions that have come out of this politicizing of crime have not always been effective. But the process itself is a healthy one in a democracy. In time, an alert electorate is going to learn what works and what doesn't work when it comes to crime-fighting promises. As Andrew von Hirsch pointed out in an ABC

News interview, political candidates taking the most simplistic stances on crime issues have not been uniformly successful in recent elections. "I think that the voters are beginning to be a little more skeptical," he said. "After all, people have run on that [toughness on crime] for ten or fifteen years, and we have toughened up and we have . . . very substantially increased the number of people that are sent to prison, and yet we don't feel safer."

If von Hirsch is right and the public is becoming better informed about the best approaches to the problem of crime, it will be more receptive to Zimring's contention that this country's excessively high level of violent crime "could be reduced gradually, particularly as we make larger social progress among the minorities" that are most affected by that violence. But the social progress that he speaks of cannot be taken for granted. It means better schools, better job training, better job opportunities. The best reason not to leave the problem of crime to the criminologists and criminal-justice professionals is that they cannot bring about these kinds of changes in society. Only an informed, reasoning public can do that.

Appendix

A tabular view of crime in the United States, based on the Federal Bureau of Investigation's Uniform Crime Report

10-Year Trend and Seasonal Fluctuations by Quarter, 1972-1981
Crime Index Total

Year	Quarter	Relative Crime Rate	Moving Average	Seasonal Relatives (percent of moving average)	Year	Quarter	Relative Crime Rate	Moving Average	Seasonal Relatives (percent of moving average)
1972	1 January-March	100	110	91.1	1977	1 January-March	116	127	91.2
	2 April-June	110	108	101.8		2 April-June	126	126	99.8
	3 July-September	116	107	108.2		3 July-September	134	126	107.0
	4 October-December	103	106	97.1		4 October-December	129	125	102.8
1973	1 January-March	97	107	90.7	1978	1 January-March	112	125	89.0
	2 April-June	108	109	99.0		2 April-June	125	127	98.9
	3 July-September	122	112	108.3		3 July-September	138	129	107.4
	4 October-December	117	116	100.6		4 October-December	134	131	102.2
1974	1 January-March	109	120	90.9	1979	1 January-March	123	133	92.5
	2 April-June	124	125	99.5		2 April-June	133	135	98.7
	3 July-September	139	130	107.3		3 July-September	146	137	106.5
	4 October-December	137	133	102.9		4 October-December	141	140	101.2
1975	1 January-March	127	135	93.9	1980	1 January-March	132	143	92.1
	2 April-June	135	137	98.2		2 April-June	146	146	100.2
	3 July-September	147	138	106.8		3 July-September	161	148	108.8
	4 October-December	141	138	102.7		4 October-December	148	148	100.1
1976	1 January-March	128	137	93.3	1981	1 January-March	140	147	95.2
	2 April-June	134	135	99.6		2 April-June	142	145	97.6
	3 July-September	142	132	107.9		3 July-September	153	*	*
	4 October-December	128	129	99.5		4 October-December	145	*	*

*Final crime data for the first and second quarters of 1982 are not available for computing moving averages and seasonal relatives for the last two quarters of 1981.

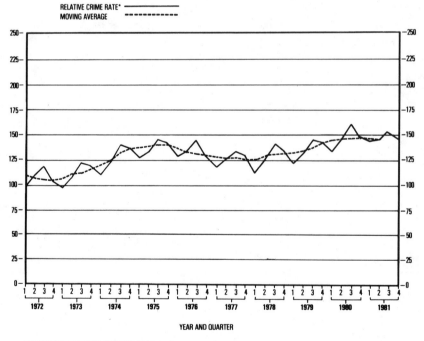

Ten-Year Trend by Quarter, 1972-1981
CRIME INDEX TOTAL

RELATIVE CRIME RATE* ————
MOVING AVERAGE ------------

YEAR AND QUARTER

*THE FIRST QUARTER OF 1972 IS EQUATED TO 100 AND IS USED AS A BASE PERIOD.

Ten-year trend in the Crime Index

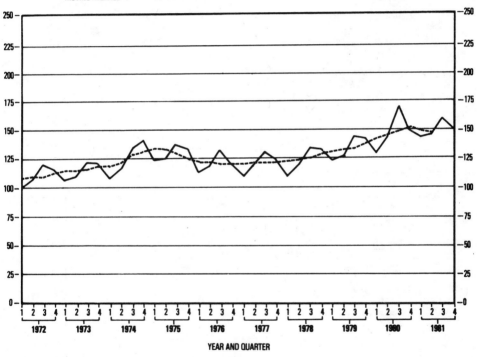

Ten-Year Trend by Quarter, 1972-1981
VIOLENT CRIME

RELATIVE CRIME RATE* ─────────
MOVING AVERAGE ─ ─ ─ ─ ─ ─ ─

YEAR AND QUARTER

*THE FIRST QUARTER OF 1972 IS EQUATED TO 100 AND IS USED AS A BASE PERIOD.

Ten-year trend in the violent-crime rate

10-Year Trend and Seasonal Fluctuations by Quarter, 1972-1981
Property Crime

Year	Quarter	Relative Crime Rate	Moving Average	Seasonal Relatives (percent of moving average)	Year	Quarter	Relative Crime Rate	Moving Average	Seasonal Relatives (percent of moving average)
1972	1 January-March	100	110	91.0	1977	1 January-March	117	128	91.1
	2 April-June	111	108	102.3		2 April-June	127	127	99.9
	3 July-September	115	106	108.0		3 July-September	135	126	107.0
	4 October-December	102	105	96.7		4 October-December	129	126	102.8
1973	1 January-March	96	106	90.5	1978	1 January-March	112	126	88.9
	2 April-June	108	109	99.2		2 April-June	126	127	99.2
	3 July-September	121	112	108.5		3 July-September	139	129	107.5
	4 October-December	116	116	100.4		4 October-December	134	131	102.1
1974	1 January-March	109	120	90.9	1979	1 January-March	123	133	92.2
	2 April-June	125	125	99.8		2 April-June	134	135	99.0
	3 July-September	140	130	107.4		3 July-September	146	137	106.5
	4 October-December	137	134	102.5		4 October-December	141	140	100.9
1975	1 January-March	127	136	93.7	1980	1 January-March	132	143	92.4
	2 April-June	136	138	98.4		2 April-June	146	146	100.3
	3 July-September	148	139	106.8		3 July-September	160	148	108.3
	4 October-December	142	139	102.5		4 October-December	148	148	100.3
1976	1 January-March	129	138	93.5	1981	1 January-March	139	146	95.3
	2 April-June	136	136	100.0		2 April-June	141	145	97.6
	3 July-September	143	133	107.8		3 July-September	153	*	*
	4 October-December	130	130	99.4		4 October-December	144	*	*

*Final crime data for the first and second quarters of 1982 are not available for computing moving averages and seasonal relatives for the last two quarters of 1981.

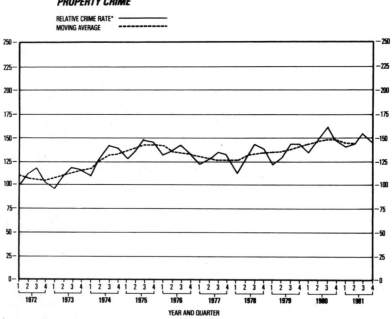

Ten-Year Trend by Quarter, 1972-1981
PROPERTY CRIME

RELATIVE CRIME RATE* ————
MOVING AVERAGE - - - - - - - -

YEAR AND QUARTER

*THE FIRST QUARTER OF 1972 IS EQUATED TO 100 AND IS USED AS A BASE PERIOD.

Ten-year trend in the property-crime rate

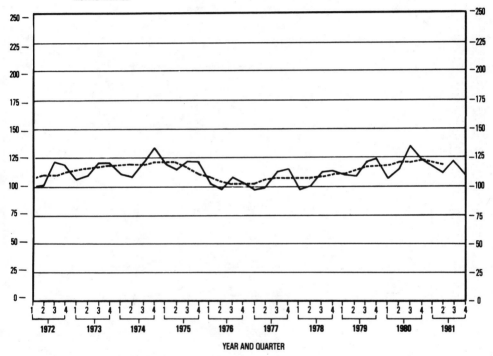

Ten-Year Trend by Quarter, 1972-1981
MURDER

RELATIVE CRIME RATE* ——————————
MOVING AVERAGE ------------

YEAR AND QUARTER

* THE FIRST QUARTER OF 1972 IS EQUATED TO 100 AND IS USED AS A BASE PERIOD.

Ten-year trend in the murder rate

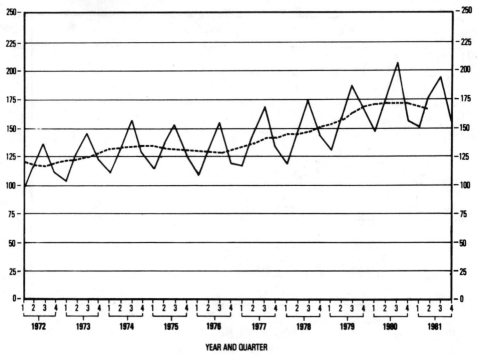

Ten-Year Trend by Quarter, 1972-1981
FORCIBLE RAPE

RELATIVE CRIME RATE* ————————
MOVING AVERAGE ---------------

YEAR AND QUARTER

*THE FIRST QUARTER OF 1972 IS EQUATED TO 100 AND IS USED AS A BASE PERIOD.

Ten-year trend in the rape rate

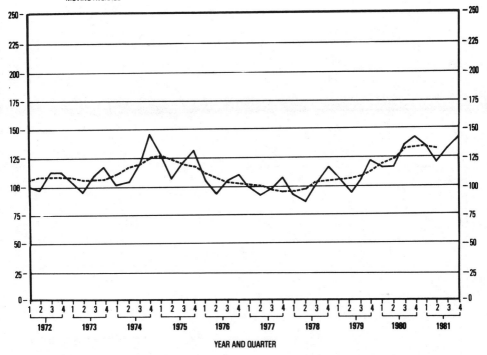

Ten-Year Trend by Quarter, 1972-1981
ROBBERY

RELATIVE CRIME RATE*
MOVING AVERAGE

YEAR AND QUARTER

*THE FIRST QUARTER OF 1972 IS EQUATED TO 100 AND IS USED AS A BASE PERIOD.

Ten-year trend in the robbery rate

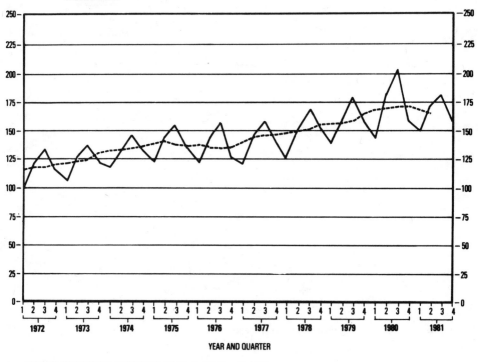

Ten-year trend in the aggravated-assault rate

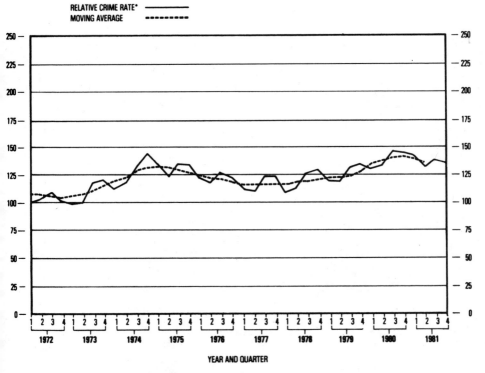

Ten-Year Trend By Quarter, 1972-1981
BURGLARY

RELATIVE CRIME RATE* ———————
MOVING AVERAGE ----------

YEAR AND QUARTER

* THE FIRST QUARTER OF 1972 IS EQUATED TO 100 AND IS USED AS A BASE PERIOD.

Ten-year trend in the burglary rate

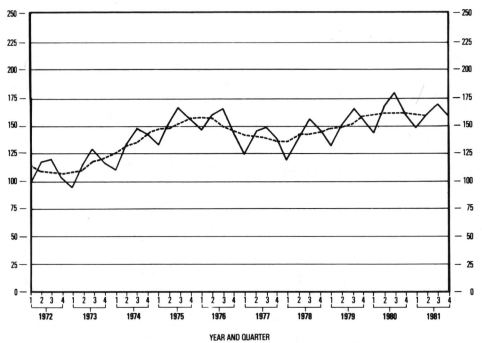

Ten-Year Trend By Quarter, 1972-1981
LARCENY - THEFT

RELATIVE CRIME RATE* ──────────
MOVING AVERAGE   ----------

YEAR AND QUARTER

* THE FIRST QUARTER OF 1972 IS EQUATED TO 100 AND IS USED AS A BASE PERIOD.

Ten-year trend in the larceny-theft rate

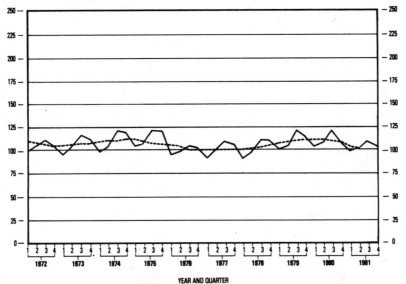

Ten-Year Trend By Quarter, 1972-1981
MOTOR VEHICLE THEFT

RELATIVE CRIME RATE*
MOVING AVERAGE

YEAR AND QUARTER

* THE FIRST QUARTER OF 1972 IS EQUATED TO 100 AND IS USED AS A BASE PERIOD.

Quarterly Seasonal Indices by Offense
Based on 1972-1981 Data

Offense	(1) January-March	(2) April-June	(3) July-September	(4) October-December	Total*
Crime Index total	92.0	99.4	107.6	101.0	400.0
Violent crime	92.3	97.2	108.0	102.5	400.0
Property crime	92.0	99.6	107.6	100.9	400.0
Murder	94.5	94.9	105.8	104.8	400.0
Forcible rape	85.7	101.9	117.8	94.7	400.0
Robbery	97.7	89.9	101.9	110.5	400.0
Aggravated assault	88.2	103.4	112.3	96.1	400.0
Burglary	96.6	95.1	104.5	103.7	400.0
Larceny-theft	89.3	102.4	109.3	98.9	400.0
Motor vehicle theft	92.6	97.3	107.1	103.1	400.0

*Indices may not add to 400.0 due to rounding.

Ten-year trend in the motor-vehicle theft rate

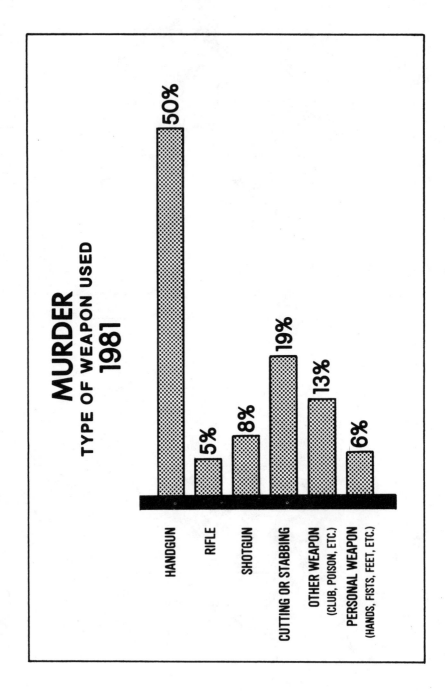

Types of weapons used in murder cases in 1981

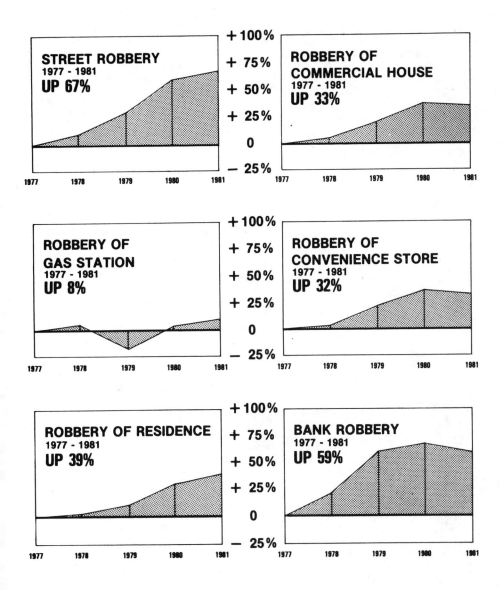

A breakdown of types of robbery in 1981

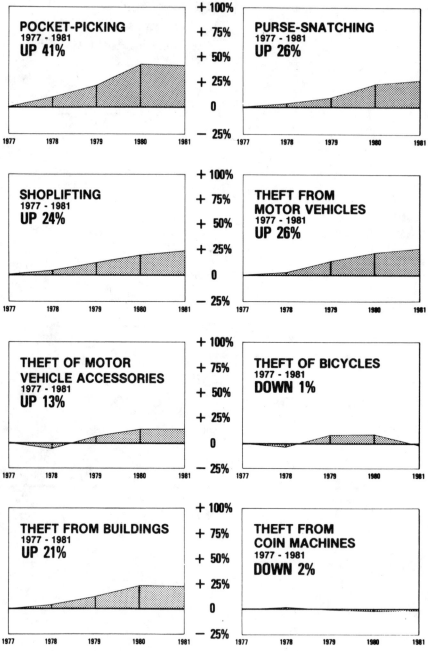

POCKET-PICKING
1977 - 1981
UP 41%

PURSE-SNATCHING
1977 - 1981
UP 26%

SHOPLIFTING
1977 - 1981
UP 24%

THEFT FROM MOTOR VEHICLES
1977 - 1981
UP 26%

THEFT OF MOTOR VEHICLE ACCESSORIES
1977 - 1981
UP 13%

THEFT OF BICYCLES
1977 - 1981
DOWN 1%

THEFT FROM BUILDINGS
1977 - 1981
UP 21%

THEFT FROM COIN MACHINES
1977 - 1981
DOWN 2%

Four-year trends in incidences of various forms of larceny

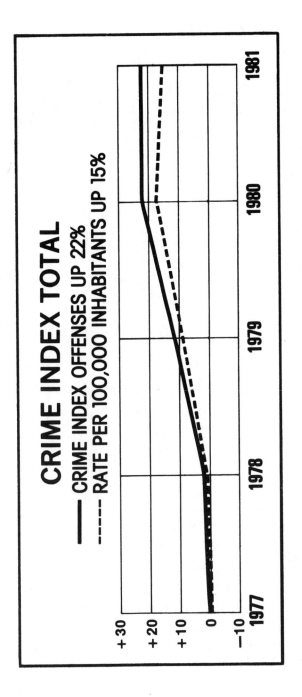

Four-year trend in the total Crime Index

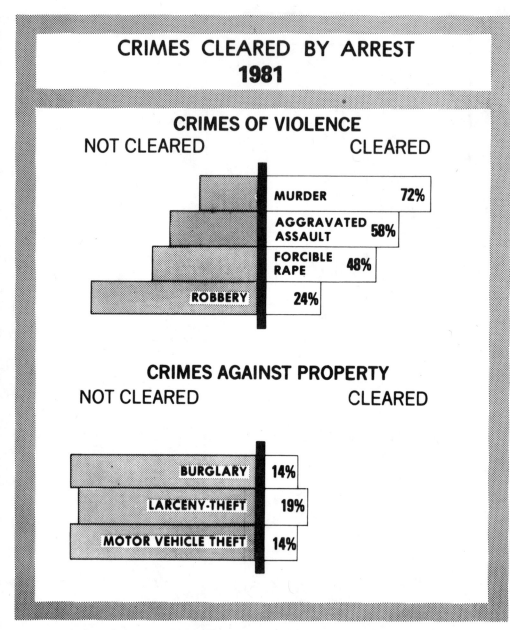

CRIMES CLEARED BY ARREST
1981

CRIMES OF VIOLENCE

NOT CLEARED   CLEARED

MURDER 72%

AGGRAVATED ASSAULT 58%

FORCIBLE RAPE 48%

ROBBERY 24%

CRIMES AGAINST PROPERTY

NOT CLEARED   CLEARED

BURGLARY 14%

LARCENY-THEFT 19%

MOTOR VEHICLE THEFT 14%

A breakdown of the frequency with which different kinds of crimes are solved or "cleared" shows police departments' low success rate with property crimes in comparison with violent crimes

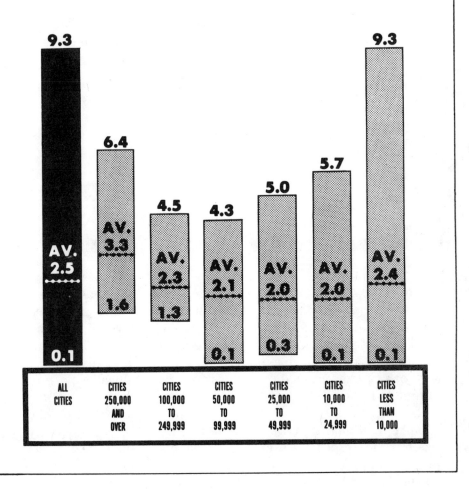

POLICE EMPLOYEE DATA

AVERAGE NUMBER OF POLICE DEPARTMENT EMPLOYEES, AND
RANGE IN NUMBER OF EMPLOYEES, PER 1,000 INHABITANTS

BY POPULATION GROUPS, 1981

9.3	6.4	4.5	4.3	5.0	5.7	9.3
AV. 2.5	AV. 3.3	AV. 2.3	AV. 2.1	AV. 2.0	AV. 2.0	AV. 2.4
0.1	1.6	1.3	0.1	0.3	0.1	0.1
ALL CITIES	CITIES 250,000 AND OVER	CITIES 100,000 TO 249,999	CITIES 50,000 TO 99,999	CITIES 25,000 TO 49,999	CITIES 10,000 TO 24,999	CITIES LESS THAN 10,000

This table shows the wide range in police-department manpower
levels among municipalities of varying sizes

Suggestions for Further Reading

Both the ABC-News personnel who worked on the Crime in America television series and the author of this book were guided in their examination of this subject by a number of books and articles. The following suggestions reflect the material that was found to be most valuable in preparing the series and this book.

For a systematic, readable discussion of virtually all aspects of crime, Charles Silberman's *Criminal Violence, Criminal Justice* [Random House, New York, 1978] is an extremely worthwhile source. Silberman's analysis of the ties connecting race and poverty with crime is especially illuminating, but his chapters on all facets of the criminal-justice system are also full of insights and carefully weighed conclusions.

Two other thought-provoking books that would serve well as introductions to the subject are Norval Morris and Gordon Hawkins' *The Honest Politician's Guide to Crime Control* [The University of Chicago Press, Chicago, 1970] and James Q. Wilson's *Thinking About Crime* [Random House, New York, 1975, originally published by Basic Books]. A far more thorough description of the criminal-justice system is to be found in Franklin E. Zimring and Richard S. Frase's *The Criminal Justice System* [Little, Brown and Company, Boston, 1980]. This volume, which is described as a course book for law-school students, will be too dense for the casual reader, but for anyone seeking an exhaustive compilation of most of the best analysis that has been done on the nation's law-enforcement system, this is it.

A somewhat dated but impressively detailed description of crime and the institutions that contend with it, including correctional facilities, can be found in *The Challenge of Crime in a Free Society: A Report by the President's Commission on Law Enforcement and the Administration of Justice* [U.S. Government Printing Office, Washington, D.C., 1967]. The passage of 16 years notwithstanding, much of its commentary, if not all of its figures, still holds up.

Two of the best volumes on the history of crime and violence in U.S. society are *The History of Violence in America: A Report to the National Commission on the Causes and Prevention of Violence*, edited by Hugh Davis Graham and Ted Robert Gurr [Frederick A. Praeger, New York, 1969] and *American Violence: A Documentary History*, edited by Richard Hofstadter and Michael Wallace [Alfred A. Knopf, New York, 1970].

Of all the volumes and reports on the problem of youth unemployment in this country, one of the most illuminating and accessible for the nonexpert is *Youth Employment and Public Policy*, edited by Bernard E. Anderson and Isabel V. Sawhill [Prentice-Hall, Englewood Cliffs, N.J., 1980].

An excellent analysis of how criminal courts function and why many attempts to change them have failed is provided by Malcolm M. Feeley's report for the Twentieth Century Fund, *Court Reform on Trial: Why Simple Solutions Fail* [Basic Books, New York, 1983]. The book is an antidote to any theories for overnight reforms of the criminal courts. Feeley's analysis of mandatory sentences is very much on target on a subject of particular concern at this time.

A more theoretical exposition of sentencing can be found in Andrew von Hirsch's Report of the Committee for the Study of Incarceration, *Doing Justice: The Choice of Punishments* [Hill and Wang, New York, 1976]. Many of the same issues are also addressed in the Report of the Twentieth Century Fund Task Force on Criminal Sentencing, *Fair and Certain Punishment*, [McGraw Hill, New York, 1976]. The background paper for this report was done by Alan M. Dershowitz. The issues discussed in both this book and von Hirsch's have been central to several states' recent initiatives to change their sentencing systems.

On the subject of juvenile crime, a good introduction to the subject is Paul A. Strasburg's report to the Ford Foundation from the Vera Institute of Justice, *Violent Delinquents* [Monarch, New York, 1978]. Strasburg is particularly useful as a guide through the sentencing alternatives for young criminals. A more theoretical discussion of some of the policy questions in handling youth crime is offered by *Confronting Youth Crime*, the Report of the Twentieth Century Task Force on Sentencing Policy Toward Young Offenders, [Holmes and Meier, New York, 1978]. Franklin E. Zimring did the background paper for this report.

The federal government turns out to be the source of one of the more informative volumes on gun-control laws. *Federal Regulation of Firearms* [Government Printing Office, Washington, D.C., 1982] is a report prepared for the Committee on the Judiciary of the U.S. Senate by the Congressional Research Service of the Library of Congress. Among its valuable features is a tabular rundown on state gun laws, as well as several articles by researchers from outside the Library of Congress on the effectiveness of gun-control laws. Steven Brill's report for the Police Foundation, *Firearm Abuse: A Research and Policy Report* [Police Foundation, Washington, D.C., 1977] remains a useful blueprint of how the 1968 Gun Control Act might still be made to accomplish some of its intended purposes.

Acknowledgments

In addition to the many outside sources acknowledged below, we would particularly like to thank the following ABC-News people for their special effort: Charles C. Stuart, Paul Friedman, Bob Roy, Sylvia Patterson, Rich O'Regan, Nancy Gabriner, John Gillen, Ray Nunn and Stu Schutzman.

We are also grateful to the individuals who helped in the conversion from a television series to this book. In particular: David O. Burbank, Frank Currie, Paul R. Desrosiers, Werner E. Elsberg, John A. Mattoon, Edward A. Sherman, Paul A. Strasburg and James Trainor.

Crime in America Special Acknowledgments

Academy for Contemporary Problems, Action for Children's Television, American Bar Association, American Civil Liberties Union, American Correctional Association, American Society of Newspaper Editors,

Arizona State University, David Armstrong, Attorneys for Criminal Justice, F. Lee Bailey, Bellevue Hospital, Prof. Alfred Blumstein, Bronx County DA's Office, Brooklyn College, Lee Brown, Allan Buono, Bureau of the Census, Bureau of Justice Statistics, Leo J. Butler, California Center for Judicial Education & Research, California Youth & Adult Correction Agency, Carnegie Mellon University, Nelson Cearlow, Center for Research on Institutions & Social Policy, Dr. Jan Chaiken, Dr. Marcia Chaiken, Chicago Crime Commission, Chicago Police Department, Citizens for Truth, Clark Foundation, Cleveland DA's Office, Clinton County Correctional Facility, Collins Correctional Facility, Columbia Journalism School, The Comedy Store, Judge Ken Cory, Crime Victims Assistance Agency, Crime Victims Task Force, Criminal Justice Publications, Dade County Juvenile Court, Dade Marine Institute, Paul Demuro, Prof. Alan Dershowitz, Detroit Police Department, Dr. Park Dietz, Eisenhower Foundation for the Prevention of Violence, Family Advocacy Council, FBI, Federal Judicial Center, Flint Police Department, Florida Environmental Institute, The Ford Foundation, Foundation for Child Development, Judge John Fox, Judge Gene Franchini, Dr. Daniel X. Friedman, Lou Ganin, Judge Seymour Gelber, Georgetown University Law Center, Judge William Gladstone, Stephen Goatlee, Adrienne Goodman, Frank Hall, Harris County DA's Office, Harvard School of Government, Harvard University, Hastings Institute, Richard Haynes, Sheriff Jack Heard, Charles Alexander Hinkle, Len Holbein, House Subcommittee on Crime, House Subcommittee on Criminal Justice, House Committee on Energy & Commerce, Houston DA's Office, Houston Police Department, Illinois Institute for Juvenile Research, Institute for Law & Social Research, Institute for Social Research, Dee & Jerry Jackson, Jefferson County DA's Office, John Jay School of Criminal Justice, David Johnston, Journal of Communication, Prof. George Kelling, Kentucky Parole Board, William Key, Bobby Kimble, Alfred Knox, Herbert Lane, Dr. Dorothy Lewis, Dr. Ner Littner, Los Angeles DA's Office, *The Los Angeles Times*, Louisville DA's Office, Marjean Martin, The Maryland Conference of Social Concern, McHugh & Hoffman, Inc., William McLeod, The Media Institute, Memphis DA's Office, Mental Health Materials Center, *Miami News*, Minnesota Sentencing Commission, Nassau County DA's Office, National Academy of Sciences, National Center for Juvenile Justice, National Center for States Courts, National Coalition on Television Violence, National Conference of State Legislatures, National Council on Crime & Delinquency, National Criminal Justice Association, National Institute of Corrections, National Institute of Justice, National Institute of Mental Health, National Office of Juvenile Justice & Delinquency Prevention, National Organization for Victim Assistance, National Prison Project, National Prison Project for the ACLU, National Victims of Crime, New York State Parole Board, New York State Youth Division, *The New York Times*, Newark Police Department, Newark Tactical Force, Northwestern Center for Urban Affairs, Northwestern University, The Patuxent Institution, Philadelphia DA's Office, Police Executive Research Forum, Police Foundation, Dr. John Pollack, President's Task Force on Victims of Crime, Prison Fellowship, Project New Pride, Dr. Richard Rada, The RAND Corporation, Research Associates, Judge John Roberts, Stephanie Roper Committee, Rural Crime Prevention Center, Rutgers University, *St. Louis Post-Dispatch*, Sam Houston School of Criminal Justice, Dr. Stanton Samenow, San Jose Police Department, Santa Ana Police Department, Rufus Sanders, Sydney Schanberg, Senate Subcommittee on Criminal Law, Judge Benjamin Shobe, Charles Silverman, Willie Smith, Robert Soshnik, Stanford University, State University of New York, Television Information Office, Dr. Hans Toch, Judge Ricardo Torres, Judge Kenneth Turner, Judge Michael Tynan, R. Emmett Tyrell, University of California, University of Chicago, University of Illinois, University of Maryland, University of Pennsylvania, University of Texas, University of Toronto, University of Virginia, University of Wisconsin, Ventura County DA's Office, Vera Institute, Victims for Victims, Violent Offenders Project, Craig Washington, Washington Journalism Center, *Washington Journalism Review*, Isaac West, Joan Williams, Yale University, Yale University Television Family Resource Center.

Index